R

A comprehensive guide to history's most famous ships of war,
spanning over 140 warships in 22 countries.

PRESERVED WARSHIPS
OF THE WORLD
N. W. (Gerry) GERHARD

Published by

MELROSE BOOKS

An Imprint of Melrose Press Limited
St Thomas Place, Ely
Cambridgeshire
CB7 4GG, UK
www.melrosebooks.com

FIRST EDITION

Copyright © N. W. Gerhard 2011

The Author asserts his moral right to
be identified as the author of this work

Typesetting and Cover designed by Matt Stephens
Cover photograph by Jay Getsinger: www.jgetsingerphotography.com

ISBN 978 1 907040 12 2

Printed and bound in Great Britain by:
CPI Antony Rowe. Chippenham, Wiltshire

FSC
www.fsc.org
MIX
Paper from
responsible sources
FSC® C013604

DEDICATION

This book is dedicated to all the crews who ever served on the ships shown for their defence of their Nation, but also to all the men who died on the many other ships also in the defence of their Nation, whichever Nation that was.

Also to my Father, Commissioned Gunner W. Gerhard RN, buried in a War Grave at Haslar Naval Cemetery, Gosport, UK and my uncle L/Telegraphist W. Evans, lost on HMS *Exmouth*, January 1940, with all hands.

May they all rest in peace.

CONTENTS

FOREWORD

Nautical history is indeed full of strange and sometimes amazing coincidences!

I was, for example, fortunate enough whilst on a business trip from West Germany to London, to coincide with the docking of Sir Francis Chichester's *Gypsy Moth* and able to go aboard to meet the great man in person.

Amazingly, after moving to Australia some 30 years later, I met and formed a close liaison with the lady who restored his previous *Gypsy I* which had foundered there earlier.

In a like manner, the history of many of the vessels portrayed in this book, carefully crafted by Gerry, my good friend of many years, is equally amazing and I am sure that all proponents, fans and preservists of these old warships will find the book engrossing.

I know that Gerry has spent many years travelling around the world to get the details and photos and has put his love of warships into the book.

Mike Neary

INTRODUCTION

As an ex-Navy man and a lover of ships, I have always felt so sad when I have seen them being towed off to the ship-breakers, so I decided about eight years ago that I would try to get photos and histories of as many ships as I could that have been preserved.

I was involved in the preservation of HMS *Belfast* in London, having worked in the engineroom whilst she was being made ready for display, and also in the raising of funds to buy HMS *Alliance*, the submarine on display at Gosport, Hampshire.

I have been to many countries in my travels, being a person with 'itchy feet', and whenever I have seen a preserved ship, I have visited her and taken photos.

I give here my deepest appreciation to all those very dedicated people, in whatever countries, who have spent so much time and labour to preserve these beautiful vessels, and have saved them for posterity and preserved them for the children who are growing up and only know them as history.

Also to the many volunteers who man these ships as guides to help the visitors with information and facts about them.

All of these people should receive a well deserved round of applause for their endeavours and dedication to this worthy cause.

Finally, I hope that this book will be a lasting memorial to these ships and help to get them recognised for the lovely vessels that they are.

Please, go and visit them, your trip will be well worth the effort and will help to maintain them.

PRESERVED WARSHIPS OF THE WORLD

Whilst many countries of the world have Navies with the ships to run them, most of the ships, when they reach the end of their useful serving life, even perhaps having served in several Navies, ultimately end up either in the wreckers' yards to be broken up, or to be scuttled as diving wrecks or targets for the use of more modern ships to try their skills or weapons on, or just to dispose of them; thus, they are lost forever. Obviously it is impossible to preserve all ships, but to those people who very often have to fight red tape and obstructionist politicians and officials, and spend many of their hours fighting to retain the ships, I dedicate this book. As an ex-Navy man and fellow ship-lover, who has spent hours on HMS *Belfast* in London helping to preserve her for posterity, I thank them from the bottom of my heart, as will all future generations to come when they tour these beautifully preserved ships and wonder at the courage, dedication and skills of the men and women who served in them so ably in the defence of their countries and of their freedom.

To the readers, I suggest that you support these wonderful people by visiting these ships and giving them the support that they need to maintain them. To all the people and officials everywhere who so ably and willingly helped me with my enquiries, I thank you, wish you all the best of luck, and hope that you can continue with your good works. I personally travelled to many countries, not only to visit and view these ships, but also to take photos for this book, and can only hope that these photos, whether taken by myself or generously donated by the guardians of these ships, will give the reader great pleasure in looking at the beautiful ships that have served their countries so well, and now rest in peace to be admired. Times change, and in the time that it has taken me to compile this book many ships may have been lost, moved or altered, and others may have been added. So, should there be any obvious alterations or additions, I would be pleased to hear about them.

Thank you for buying and reading my book, and I hope that it gives you as much pleasure in looking at these remnants of past ages, so well preserved by their loving and dedicated carers, as it has been for me to compile this record.

The author gratefully acknowledges the help given to him by people and establishments who have donated some of the photos, and therefore gives the photos the credit due to them and those people and establishments, with the copyright being due to them. All other photos shown are those taken by the author in his travels around the world in the compiling of this book and remain his copyright. Some of the locations of the ships and their appearances may have changed since the book was compiled, due to changing times and fortunes; however, it was up to date at the time I started to write it and the laying out of the photos. Should the readers have any relevant material then I would be most grateful if they could contact me via the publishers.

Copyright N. W. (Gerry) Gerhard, 2006.

Plate 1 – The fate of many warships; the wrecker's yard. Here at a wrecker's at Portsmouth lie the remains of HM ships Russell, Virago *and an 'A' class submarine to be broken up.*

Plate 2 – Old cannons used as traffic bollards at Portsea, Portsmouth UK. (Author's collection.)

PART ONE
UNITED STATES OF AMERICA

BATTLESHIPS, CARRIERS, CRUISERS, DESTROYERS, SUBMARINES PRESERVED WARSHIPS IN THE USA

The USA has probably the largest, most comprehensive, collection of preserved warships in the world, ranging from battleships down to submarines, and the dedicated people who have been instrumental in saving these ships are to be congratulated on their hard work and perseverance to bring these ships to the beautiful condition that they are now in. My thanks go to all those lovely people in the USA who have helpfully assisted me with photos, histories and details of those ships. I have listed them here, but should I have inadvertently missed anyone out, then I humbly apologise and say "thank you" now to them and all the helpers.

USS *CONSTELLATION*

This is the oldest warship still afloat in the world, and is now not in active service in the US Navy, unlike her sister ship, USS *Constitution*. She is beautifully preserved as a Historical National Shrine at Pratt Street in Baltimore. She was launched on 7th September 1797, after being laid down in 1794 under a bill called for by President George Washington, one of six frigates to be built, and was launched very shortly before the *Constitution*, but only three of the projected six were eventually built. She was built in Baltimore, where she now lies, by David Stodders Fells Point shipyard, and was first sailed under the command of Captain Thomas Truxton on 26th June 1798. She first saw action in February 1799 against the French *L'Insurgente* and again, a year later, against the French *La Vengeance*. Later, she served in the Mediterranean and the Pacific and later still in Africa, where she helped to break up the slave trade. After a spell of neglect, she was rather forgotten and misused until President F. D. Roosevelt recalled her to duty for her country again as a relief static flagship of the US Atlantic fleet in the Second World War. From that time on she never looked back and is lovingly cared for and visited by millions of people every year, a noble resting place and duty for a very proud and wonderful ship of her age.

Contact details:

US Frigate *Constellation*, Pier 1. C/o Harbourmaster's Office, Pratt St, Baltimore, Maryland, 21202, USA.

USS *CONSTITUTION*

This is the second oldest warship still afloat and is still officially on the register of the US Navy as a serving warship, and is still in full commission. She is lovingly known as 'Old Ironsides', a name that she received when she was involved in a battle with HMS *Guerriere* on 19th August 1812, when the British ship fired a long range shot at her and the shot fell into the sea after glancing off her sides. She was launched in 1797, very shortly after her sister ship, USS *Constellation*, and is at present the flagship of the Commandant of the first Naval district. She is normally moored outside of the main gates of the Naval yard at Boston Naval shipyard in Charleston, Massachusetts, and frequently puts to sea. She was chosen by the Post Office Department in 1964 as one of the three symbols of US heritage, along with the *Eagle* and the *Liberty Bell*, to appear on a four-cent blue-stamped envelope. She is one of Boston's leading tourist attractions and is also visited by many foreign visitors. She is in a very beautiful condition and is a credit to the US Navy and the United States of America for the way she is maintained. See plates 3, 4 and 5 on Page 3.

Plate 3 – *USS* Constitution *at Boston Naval Shipyard, Charleston National Park, Massachusetts. (Photo courtesy of US Navy Office of Information.)*
Plate 4 – *Mainmast of the* Constitution *being replaced in 1980. (Photo courtesy of US Navy Office of Information.)*
Plate 5 – *USS* Constellation. *(Photo courtesy of US Navy Office of Information.)*

USS *MISSOURI* (BB63) *The Mighty Mo*

The keel of the *Missouri* was laid down on 6th January 1941, at New York Navy Yard, Brooklyn and she was launched on 29th January 1944, and finally commissioned on 11th June 1944, becoming operational on 14th December. She is the fourth ship and the second battleship to bear this State's name. She is one of the Iowa class of five battleships, although six were originally started and *Illinois* was cancelled when 22% completed in August 1945, due to the end of the Second World War, and *Kentucky* was 69.2% completed when work stopped. Both *Illinois* and *Kentucky* were finally scrapped. These were the largest class of battleship to be built for the US Navy.

Technical specifications:

The standard displacement is of 45,000 tonnes (58,000 tonnes war load) with a complement of 2,700 men. Her guns are 9 x 16" x 50 cal in three turrets (with a range of twenty-three miles), 20 x 5" x 38 cals (with a range of nine miles), 80 x 40mm and over 40 x 20mm and machine guns; later she carried four Vulcan Phalanx weapons systems, thirty-two Tomahawk missiles and sixteen Harpoon anti-surface missiles. She also carried four or more aircraft and two catapults. Her machinery is by Gen. Electric Co., with geared turbines to four shafts, SHP 180,000 = thirty-three knots. Twelve Babcock & Wilcox boilers burning fuel oil. Her overall length is 887.3ft, beam of 108.3ft and a draught of 38ft at full load with an overall height of 209.8ft.

She holds the distinction, amongst others, of being the last of the battleships to be commissioned into the US Navy, and also that she was, in 1992, the last operational

3

battleship in the world. She was a mighty ship and provided supporting groundfire for many famous battles in the Second World War, and served at Iwo Jima, Okinawa and the Pacific raids of 1945. On 2nd September 1945, she was chosen to be the ship to take the final surrender of the Japanese forces and the signing of the Formal Instrument of Surrender of that nation. The signing of this historic document was the end of the world's worst and bloodiest war in history. She now carries a plate on her quarterdeck to commemorate this moment in history. Before her de-commissioning on 26th February 1955, she participated in several bombardments during the Korean War, between 1950 and 1953. On 10th May 1986 she was re-commissioned and went on a round-the-world cruise, making her the first battleship to circle around the world since 'The Great White Fleet', which President T. Roosevelt had sent in 1907 to 1909. In 1987 she was sent to the Persian Gulf to protect American tankers near the Strait of Hormuz. In 1988, she also partook in The Rim of the Pacific Exercise, off the Hawaiian Islands. In 1991, *Missouri* was sent to the Persian Gulf War and there she fired her range of Tomahawk missiles and bombarded shore targets to use up her 16" ammunition.

Plate 6 – *A view taken from the jetty of the stern section of USS* Missouri *(BB63), moored at Pearl Harbour, Hawaii. (Author's collection.)*
Plate 7 – *The forward triple 16" gun turrets. (Author's collection.)*
Plate 8 – *Looking forward from the bridge of* Missouri *over her turrets is the USS* Arizona *Memorial, which is just forward of USS* Missouri. *(Author's collection.)*

On 31st March 1991, she was de-commissioned for the last time in her very illustrious career, and in 1995 she was finally struck from the Naval Ships Register. It was decided that the 'Mighty Mo' should be preserved for posterity as a memorial museum. The USS *Missouri* Memorial Association Inc. of Hawaii was selected to have the sole responsibility of preserving this great piece of the United States Navy, and, in 1998, the 'Mighty Mo' reached her final resting place at Ford Island, the historic place where so many US battleships had been damaged and sunk by the Japanese at Pearl Harbour in Hawaii, and near to where one of her sisters (as a battleship, not a class), the USS *Arizona,* sunk on 7th December 1941, and now a sad memorial to the men and women who lost their lives on that 'Day of Infamy'. USS *Missouri* now lies at peace as a museum ship and the author went over her and found that she had been preserved in excellent condition and is a credit to her loving carers, well worth visiting if you are in the area. There is a bus that will take you directly to the wharf where she is moored.

Contact details:

USS *Missouri* Memorial Association Inc., PO Box 6339, Honolulu, Hawaii, 96818. Telephone: (808) 423 2263 – Fax: (808) 423 0700 – Toll Free (888) 877 6477 ext. 2. Reservations: (877) 644 4896.
Website: www.ussmissouri.org

Plate 9 – *Remembrance plaque for signing of the end of War on* Missouri. *(Author's collection.)*
Plate 10 – *The view from the jetty and entrance area of the bridge and the bow section. (Author's collection.)*
Plate 11 – *USS* Missouri *at her final resting place in Pearl Harbour. (Author's collection.)*

USS *NEW JERSEY* (BB62)

The *New Jersey* is a battleship of the 'Iowa' class and one of her sister ships is the USS *Missouri*, which is preserved at Hawaii (see Page 3).

She is preserved at Camden, New Jersey. She was laid down at Philadelphia Navy Yard on 16th September 1940, launched on 7th December 1940 and commissioned on 23rd May 1943. During the Second World War, she fired 771 rounds from her main battery and in two deployments off Korea she fired 6,671 rounds. During her deployment off Vietnam, she fired 5,688 rounds of her 16" main battery guns and a total of 6,200 rounds altogether, the extra rounds being for tests and training. She also fired over 15,000 rounds from her 5" secondary guns. She was, like her sister ships, fitted out as a Fleet Flagship with additional accommodations and bridge level for an admiral and staff. When built, they carried three float planes, but these were later removed and replaced with helicopters. This class of ship was the most heavily armoured US warship ever built, the main armour belt was 12.1" thick, the lower armour belt, aft of turret three to protect the propellers, was 13.5". Turret faces are 17", tops are 7.25" and backs are 12".

USS *New Jersey* participated in nearly all of the Western Pacific campaigns from her arrival in the theatre in January 1944 until the end of the Second World War. Her first combat action came as a unit of the Fifth Fleet in assaults on the Marshall Islands. Next was the invasion of the Marianas where her heavy guns battered Saipan and Tinian. She screened carriers as American and Japanese pilots duelled in the Battle of the Philippine Sea, and then contributed to strikes on Guam and the Palaus. In October 1944, she was Admiral William Halsey's 3rd Fleet flagship during the Battle of Leyte Gulf – the world's largest Naval battle – and accompanied Allied Naval forces to waters off the Philippines, Okinawa and Formosa in 1945.

New Jersey was directly engaged in the conquest of Okinawa in early 1945. She fought off air raids, rescued downed pilots and defended the carriers from Kamikaze suicide planes. *New Jersey* also provided heavy bombardment, preparing the beaches for Allied invasion forces. Following flagship assignments in Japanese waters in late 1945, she took aboard nearly a thousand homeward-bound troops returning to the US.

In 1946, The 'Big J' returned to the Atlantic, making midshipman cruises to northern European waters and operating in the western Atlantic. She was de-commissioned at Bayonne, NJ in June 1948. With the outbreak of hostilities in Korea, she was re-commissioned on 21st November 1950. During her two tours of duty in Korean waters, she operated in direct support of United Nations troops, interdicting Communist supply and communication routes. During her first shore bombardment mission at Wonsan, she received her only combat casualty in her forty-eight years of service when a crewman was killed and three wounded by Communist shore battery fire.

New Jersey made deployments to Northern Europe and the Mediterranean between 1955 and her de-commissioning at Bayonne on 21st August 1957. Her third career began on 6th April 1968 when she was re-commissioned in Philadelphia. Operating from her new home port of Long Beach, California, as the world's only active battleship, she arrived off the coast of Vietnam in late 1968. The Department of Defence later estimated that one hundred American servicemen's lives were saved for each day she served off the coast of Vietnam, destroying enemy gun positions, troop concentrations and supply areas. *New Jersey* was de-commissioned for the third time at the Puget Sound Naval Shipyard on 17th December 1969.

New Jersey returned to the active fleet for the final time in December 1982. After mounting a show of strength off troubled El Salvador, she rushed to the Mediterranean in the fall of 1983 to provide fire support for Marines in Beirut, Lebanon. The first US Navy warship to fire a Tomahawk cruise missile or enter the Persian Gulf, the 'Big J' served in a variety of roles, including regular deployments to the Western Pacific. She was de-commissioned for the fourth and final time in February 1991, after travelling more miles and firing more shells than any other battleship in history. As America's most decorated surviving warship, *New Jersey* has been meticulously restored to her 1990 appearance, and opened for tours in October 2001. Today, as the most modern and complete missile-armed museum warship open to the public anywhere in the world, visitors can experience the only floating, interactive Combat Engagement Centre (CEC) depicting modern Naval warfare at sea on its docent-led Firepower Tour, an up close and detailed look at the impressive weapon systems onboard the 'Big J'. *New Jersey* also offers regular docent-guided tours and self-guided tours, each covering seven decks, including the flag and navigation bridges, wardroom, enlisted sleeping quarters, galley and mess decks. All tours feature *New Jersey's* fully restored *Seasprite* anti-submarine helicopter and massive 16" and 5" guns. All tours include full colour, large, extensive interpretive signage as well as video and other interactive elements for its guests, and several permanent and rotating interactive exhibits. Host your next meeting, conference, tradeshow, social event or class reunion onboard America's most decorated battleship! Permanently berthed along the Camden Waterfront, *New Jersey* also boasts an extensive overnight encampment program, and a shore-side 4-D Flight Simulator depicting her Second World War 'Seahawk' gunnery spotter aircraft in action off Okinawa.

Contact details:

For the Battleship: 100 Clinton Street, Camden, ND 08103, USA.
For the Parking Garage: 2 Riverside Drive, Camden, N3 08103, USA.

My grateful thanks to Jason Hall, of the VP Curatorial Affairs and Education on USS *New Jersey* for his help and information.

USS *NORTH CAROLINA* (BB55)

This battleship is of the Washington Class Programme of 1936 and was laid down on 27th October 1937 at New York Navy Yard at a cost of $70,885,750. She was launched on 13th June 1940, commissioned on 9th April 1941 and completed six years' service. She is the third ship in the US Navy by that name (see below for details on the first ship to be named *North Carolina*).

Technical specifications:

Her standard displacement was 35,000 tonnes (load 41,000 tonnes) and her complement was 2,500 men. She is 729ft long overall, with a beam of 108ft and draught of 26ft 8". She has 9 x 16" guns in three triple turrets, which were of a new design at the time of her building, weighing 125 tonnes each, and each turret weighs 650 tonnes. She has 20 x 5" x 38 cal dual purpose guns and over 100 x 40mm and 20mm AA guns. She carried four aircraft with two catapults and her armour is 16" amidships and 6" upper and lower decks. She has a triple hull below the waterline. Her machinery is by General Electric Co., comprising four shaft geared turbines, SHP of 115,000 = over twenty-seven knots, and has Babcock & Wilcox boilers with a reported working pressure of about 600lb PSI and 400 degrees of superheat. She had a crew of 2,000 officers and men.

There were delays in her building due to changes in design and in materials being delivered, but she has a 35% fully welded hull construction. The engine room was arranged in a new planned layout to save weight. Her steam pressures and temperatures were reported to be greater than any other battleship afloat at that time. Her sister ship in the class was USS *Washington* (Class name ship) and she was scrapped in 1961. *North Carolina* is the third ship to carry the name of the State. During the Second World War she earned twelve battle stars and was torpedoed by the Japanese submarine *I-15* and had a hole 32ft long and 18ft high blown in her, but she survived this blow and was repaired to return to the War and serve in all the major campaigns in the Pacific, notably Guadalcanal Landings, Eastern Solomons, Gilbert Islands, Kwajalein Truk, Saipan, Philippines, Iwojima, in the North Atlantic 1941 and the Pacific raids 1945. She was affectionately known as 'The Showboat' and is still known by that name to this day. She was de-commissioned on 27th June 1947 and put into the first class reserve fleet at Bayonne NL, but when she was struck from the Navy List and it was decided to scrap her, she was offered to the State of North Carolina and a fund was then raised to purchase her for a memorial. When the amount of $250,000 was raised she was purchased, and on September 1961 she started on her final voyage under tow, and on 2nd October 1961 she came up Cape Fear River and was manoeuvred (after going aground once) into the Port of Wilmington, where she now lies as a permanent memorial to the brave sailors and ships of the United States Navy. Her sister ship *Washington* was scrapped at Newark (USA) in October 1961.

The first *North Carolina* was a ship of the line built at the Philadelphia Shipyard. The keel was laid down in 1818 and she was launched in late 1820 and then completed in the Norfolk shipyard in 1824. She was 193ft long, displaced 2,633 tonnes and had seventy-four guns. She was finally sold in 1867 for $30,000. Her original figurehead was of Sir Walter Raleigh and was given to the State of North Carolina in 1909, where presumably it still is today. During the American Civil War the Confederate States Navy had a 150ft long sloop named North Carolina. Built at Wilmington, *North Carolina* never got out of the Cape Fear River and on 27th September 1864, she sank there. The second US Naval vessel to be named North Carolina was an armoured cruiser number twelve and was built by the Newport News Shipbuilding and Drydock Company, launched on 5th October 1906 and commissioned on 7th May 1908. Length (overall) was 504.6ft, with a beam of 72.11ft; she displaced 14,500 tonnes with a speed of twenty-two knots. She had four x 10" guns and fifty-six smaller guns. In the First World War she made six round trips to Europe. On 5th November 1915, she made the first ever catapult launching of an aircraft whilst underway. She was finally paid off and sold for scrap on 29th September 1930.

This *North Carolina* joined the Fleet on 9th April 1941 and was the first battleship to be commissioned since 1923. She saw much war service, first at Guadalcanal and then at Tulagi. At the battle of the Eastern Solomons, she shot down seven enemy aircraft and on 15th September 1942, a torpedo fired by the Japanese submarine *I-15,* at the destroyer *Lansdowne*, missed but struck the *North Carolina*. The explosion killed four men and wounded twenty-three; it tore a hole in her and she developed a five degree list. She returned to Pearl Harbour for repairs and was there from 30th September to 17th November 1942. She returned again on 27th March 1943 for repairs and some alterations and then headed for Noumea, New Caledonia, where she arrived on 27th May. After operating there for some months, she again returned to Pearl Harbour to prepare for the Gilbert Islands operations. There she joined the Saratoga Carrier Group and fired 538 x 16" shells. On 25th December 1943 she sailed for New Ireland and then to Funa Futi in the Ellice Islands. She was then involved in the action and invasion of the Marshall Islands and then at Truk, Guam and Saipan. At Saipan she shot down another enemy plane. Then she was involved in the Western New Guinea landings and the invasion of the Marianas Islands, where she got another enemy plane. She put 158 x 16" shells into Ponape Island and then returned to Hawaii for rudder repairs, which were completed on 24th May. She then spent several months in the Pacific area and off Okinawa, where she got three more enemy aircraft but suffered a hit from 'friendly' fire; a 5" AA shell, which hit a gun director, killing three men and wounding forty-four more. She entered Tokyo Bay on 5th September 1945 and then headed home to reach Boston on 17th October 1945. Altogether, she had steamed 307,000 miles, entered twenty-six ports, shot down twenty-four enemy planes, sunk a merchantman, had twelve battle stars awarded to her and had only seventy-three men killed or wounded; a proud record indeed. She was finally de-commissioned on 27th June 1947.

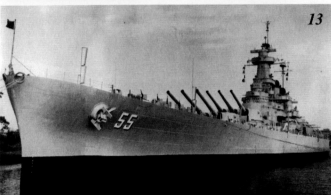

Plate 12 – USS North Carolina *at Wilmington.*
Plate 13 – USS North Carolina. *Photos courtesy of the USS Battleship commission.*

USS *MASSACHUSETTS* (BB59)

This battleship is one of the four ships of the South Dakota class, and was built at Bethlehem Steel Co. (Quincy) in the State for which she was named. She was laid down on 20th July 1939 and completed in September 1942 at a cost of $77 million.

Technical specifications:

She has a standard displacement of 35,000 tonnes and fully loaded (wartime) of 42,000 tonnes. She carried a complement of 2,500 men. Length is 680ft, beam 108.2ft and draught is 26.9ft. Machinery four shaft geared turbines. SHP 130,000 = thirty knots, boilers by Babcock & Wilcox at a working pressure of 600lb per square inch with 400 degrees of superheat and was oil-fired. She carried, in wartime, 9 x 16" guns in three triple turrets, 16 x 5" x 38 cal dual purpose, and over 100 x 40 and 20mm, four or more aircraft and two catapults. She had heavy side armour comparable to the previous Washington class of battleship, of which this class is a modification (see USS *North Carolina*).

She now lies preserved at Battleship Cove, Fall River, Massachusetts. She is credited with having fired the first and last 16" shells by an American warship in the Second World War, the first as flagship for 'Operation Torch' and the last at the Japanese Island of Honshu in 1945, and during this time she took part in many American operations and landings throughout the Pacific where she was based. She also played a prominent part in the Naval victory over the Japanese squadron in the Battle of Guadalcanal on 13th to 15th November 1942. Her pennant no. is BB59 and at the end of her service career she was put up for disposal in 1962 and struck from the Navy Register and was then purchased by the State to be preserved for posterity. She arrived from Norfolk VA, where she had been lying in reserve, on 12th June 1965 and was opened to the public for the first time on 31st July 1965, since when she has received many visitors. The State of Massachusetts is to be well applauded in their action of buying her to be preserved and the very good condition that they are maintaining her in.

Contact details:

USS *Massachusetts* Memorial Committee Inc., Battleship Cove, Fall River, Massachusetts 02721, USA.

Plate 14 – Also preserved here are the PT Boats Nos. 73 and 79 and a portion of the bow of USS Fall River. *Battleship USS* Massachusetts, *the submarine USS* Lionfish *and the Destroyer USS* Joseph P. Kennedy Jr. *Now preserved at Fall River, Massachusetts. (Photo courtesy of the State of Massachusetts.)*

Please see destroyer and submarine sections for details of *Lionfish* and *Kennedy*. Pages 36 and Page 28.

USS *ALABAMA* (BB60)

The *Alabama* is of the South Dakota class, a sister ship and similar to the *Massachusetts* (Page 11). She was laid down on 1st February 1940 at Norfolk Navy Yard with machinery installed by the Westinghouse Co., but in all other aspects, she is the same as the others in this class.

Commissioned on 16th August 1942, the USS *Alabama* (BB60) spent a total of forty months in active service in the Pacific theatre of the Second World War. In that time, she fought through twenty-six engagements and operations, earning nine battle stars on her Asiatic-Pacific Theatre Campaign Ribbon and served with the British Home Fleet 1943, Gilbert Islands, Kwajalein, Truk, Marianas, Palau, Leyte Gulf, Okinawa and the Pacific Raids 1945. She completed an initial tour of duty protecting lend-lease convoys to Britain and Russia while operating with the British Home Fleet before joining the Third Fleet in the Pacific. From that point on, her itinerary reads like a listing of the battles of the Pacific, since there were few in which she didn't take part. The culmination of her battle career came when she bombarded engineering works on the Japanese Island of Honshu, some fifty miles north of Tokyo. Despite heavy rain, which restricted visibility, the *Alabama* demolished the targets assigned to her. Her final mission was the embarkation of 700 passengers at Okinawa for the trip home.

After the Second World War, she spent seventeen years in the Bremerton Group of the Reserve Fleet. She was presented to the state of Alabama in 1964 and moored at her present site off the Mobile, Alabama, Ship Channel. Battleship Park, which also includes the submarine USS *Drum* (SS-228), is an all-service memorial to the veterans of the Second World War and the Korean War.

Contact details:

USS *Alabama* Battleship Commission, Battleship Park, PO Box 65, Mobile, Alabama, 36601, USA.
Telephone: (251) 433 2703. Fax: (251) 433 2777
E-mail: btunnell@ussalabama.com
Website: www.ussalabama.com
Also preserved here is USS *Drum* SS 228 (see Page 33).

Plate 15 – USS *Alabama*.
Plate 16 – Photos courtesy
of USS Battleship *Alabama*
Commission.
Plate 17 – The forward triple 16"
turrets of USS *Alabama*.

USS *TEXAS* (BB35)

USS *Texas* is of the New York Class of two ships. She was authorised in 1910 and laid down in April 1911 and was launched on 18th May 1912 and completed in March 1914. She is the third ship named after the State.

Technical specifications:

Built at Newport News shipyard, her displacement was 27,000 tonnes (32,000 at full load) with a length of 573ft overall, beam of 106ft and draught of 31.5ft full load. Her guns are 10 x 14" x 45 cal, 6 x 5" x 51 cal, 8 x 3" x 50 cal and later, many 40 x 20mm AA guns. She has a catapult on the midships turret and her armour ranged from 12" down to 3" on the deck. Her machinery was put in by her builders and is vertical triple expansion, four cylinder x two shafts. SHP = 28,100 = twenty-one knots. Six Bureau Express boilers and she had an oil carrying capacity of 5,200 tonnes.

She joined the sixth battle squadron and in February 1918 she fired her first of many salvos at the enemy. Between the two World Wars, she became the first battleship to launch an aircraft from her deck when a Sopwith Camel was flown off a wooden runway platform on her number two turret. She had a new fire control system installed in 1926 and a tripod foremast was also fitted. She cruised in Mexican waters to uphold US rights against General Huerta. She also cruised with the British Grand Fleet in the First World War, when the US eventually declared war on Germany. On the outbreak of the Second World War, on 3rd September 1939, she took part in neutrality patrols in the North Atlantic. When Germany declared war on the US she then went to war stations and was involved with the Allied task force that landed 35,000 troops in North Africa after the British defeat of Rommel. She also took part in the Normandy landings on D-Day, bombarding the shore batteries of the Germans there. Early in 1945 she was in the Pacific, bombarding Iwo Jima and Okinawa. When Japan surrendered, she then returned to the US where she sailed to Galveston. She was then put into a State of Reserve but her future looked bleak and it seemed likely that she would end up in the breaker's yard, but Admiral Hutchinson asked Fleet Admiral Nimitz (both Texans) to have her presented to the State of Texas, which Nimitz requested and approval was given for her to become a State shrine. On 21st April 1948 she was moved into a slip off the Houston Ship Canal and so became the first battleship to be preserved and enshrined by a State.

Contact details:

Battleship *Texas*, 10575 Katy Freeway, STE 393, Houston, Texas, 77024, USA.

Also enshrined with her is the Second World War submarine *Cabrilla* (SS288), details of which are listed on Page 36.

18

Plate 18 – *USS* Texas *at the San Jacinto State Park. (Photo courtesy of The Battleship* Texas *Commission.)*

Plate 19 – *USS* Texas *at the San Jacinto State Park. (Photo courtesy of The Battleship* Texas *Commission.)*

USS *WISCONSIN* (BB64)

At the Naval Museum, Hampton Roads, Norfolk, Virginia, USA lies the Second World War Battleship *Wisconsin*. At the time of writing (October 2009) she still remains in ready reserve status in the US Navy, but, in a few months to come, she will be transferred under the Navy's ship donation programme and will then become a museum ship at Norfolk in the Hampton Roads Naval Museum. At the moment she is moored alongside the jetty and people are allowed on to the weather decks only to tour her, but when she is donated she will become fully open to visitors as a museum ship. She can also, at the moment, be used for ceremonies aboard, i.e. weddings, reunions, memorial services etc. as well as military ceremonies.

BB64 is the second ship in the US fleet to carry the name; the first was BB9, laid down in 1898 and commissioned in 1901 and of the Alabama class with a displacement of 11,565 tonnes. This second ship cost $110 million to build. She is of the Iowa class, with her preserved sister ships.

Like *Missouri* (BB63 at Hawaii, see Page 3) and *New Jersey* (BB62 at Camden, New Jersey, see Page 7) she was built at Philadelphia AA/Westinghouse Yard, laid down on 25th January 1941, launched on 7th December 1943 and commissioned on 16th April 1944. She joined Task Force 58 in the Pacific on 17th November 1944, de-commissioned for the first time on 1st July 1948 and then re-commissioned on 3rd March 1951. She joined Task Force 77 in Korea on 1st December 1951, was hit by a North Korean shell on 15th March 1952, with three crew members injured, and was involved in a collision with USS *Eaton* (DD510) on 6th May 1956. She was de-commissioned on 8th March 1958 and then re-commissioned on 22nd October 1988. She then joined Battle Force 'Zulu' in the Persian Gulf on 1st September 1990, and was finally de-commissioned on 30th September 1991. She arrived in downtown Norfolk on 7th December 2000 and opened to the public on 16th April 2001.

Technical specifications:

887.3ft x 108.2ft x 37.8ft, displacement 45,000 tonnes, speed thirty-three knots. Machinery: eight Babcock & Wilcox 600PSI boilers. Four Westinghouse steam turbines, HP 212,000 SHP, two five-bladed (17.5") and two (18.3") four-bladed propellers. Her armour is main belt 12.1" tapering down to 1.62". Turret 17" to 7.25". Armament is nine 16" guns cal MK7 in three turrets and twelve 5" cal 38 in twin mounts. Later she was fitted with thirty-two Tomahawk missiles in eight MK 143 launchers and sixteen Harpoon missiles in four MK 141 quad launchers. During the 'Desert Storm' action she fired a total of twenty-four Tomahawk missiles and delivered 120 tonnes of high explosive shells on land targets. Her 16" guns can fire a 1,900 or 2,700 pound shell and need six 110 lb bags of cordite to do this and can reach a range of up to twenty-three nautical miles.

Contact details:

Hampton Roads Naval Museum, Suite 248, 1 Waterside Drive, Norfolk, VA 23510 1607, USA.

Telephone: (757) 445 8971. Fax: (757) 445 1867.

General information: 757 322 2987 and 2988. Reception and catering: (757) 664 1012 or (757) 664 1042. Historical information: 757 322 2993 or 322 2984.

USS *Wisconsin* Association: www.usswisconsin.org

Battleship *Wisconsin* Foundation: www.battleshipwisconsin.org

Naval Museum: www.hrnm.navy.mil Disabled access arranged. Admission is free. No smoking is allowed on board. Public parking is available and city parking at nominal hourly rates.

The author would like to express his thanks to the Curator, Joseph M. Judge, for his great help with details and the photo provided.

The Badger, Wisconsin's monthly newspaper, reported the following figures in its October 1945 issue. During the Second World War, Wisconsin crewmen consumed on a daily basis (with a total complement exceeding 3,100 officers and men):

Twenty tonnes of food provisions consumed in one week:

4,110 pounds of vegetables; 1,640 pounds of fruit; 1,500 pounds of flour; 2,465 pounds of meat; 1,200 pounds of potatoes; 164 pounds of butter; 6,500 eggs; 217.5 gallons of ice cream (an additional 3,500 quarts were transferred to other ships in the task force in May 1944); 275 bars of Ivory Soap; 2,000 gallons of coffee (an additional 1,500 pounds were transferred to other ships in the task force in May 1944.)

To get *Wisconsin* to sea, it took 6,250 shipbuilders; 2,500,000 man hours to design; 30,000,000 man hours to build; 312,000 pounds of paint; 5,000 electric light bulbs; 348,000 pounds of blueprint *pa;* 1,135,000 rivets; 4,300,000 feet of welding; 1,330,000 feet of electric cable; 422,000 feet of piping; nine-and-a-half acres of deck; and 900 electric motors.

Plate 20 – *USS* Wisconsin. *(Photo courtesy of Joseph M. Judge.)*

USS *IOWA*

Plate 21 – *Now de-commissioned, shown alongside at South Railway Jetty Portsmouth on a goodwill visit. (Photo courtesy of Ian A. White.)*

USS *NIAGARA*

This ship was the relief flagship of Commodore Oliver Hazard Perry (after whom a class of forty-eight US frigates was named in 1975) in the battle of Lake Erie on 10th September 1813, and was the 110ft long Brig Niagara of twenty guns.

She was lost in Misery Bay near Erie and her remains were eventually found and recovered a hundred years after the battle. She has been fully reconstructed to her original condition by the Commonwealth of Pennsylvania. She is now lying on land at the foot of State St, Erie, Pa, preserved for all time, and can be visited there. After transferring his flag from USS *Lawrence* to USS *Niagara*, Perry had inscribed on it the very famous words of Captain James Lawrence, "Don't give up the ship!" and he then went on to win a victory in this ship. She has been very well restored and is a credit to the many people who have devoted much of their time to preserving her.

22

Plate 22 – *USS* Niagara *preserved at State St, Erie, Pa. (Photo courtesy of Commonwealth of Pennsylvania.)*

USS *OLYMPIA*

This old US cruiser is now moored as a museum ship at Philadelphia's Penn's Landing. She was laid down at San Francisco in June 1891 and launched on November 1892 and then completed and commissioned on 5th February 1895. She was the sole member of her class.

Technical specifications:

Her overall length is 325ft, with a beam of 53ft and a draught of 25ft, carrying a crew of 166 men. Her displacement was 5,870 tonnes and she has 4 x 8" x 35 cal guns, 10 x 5" x 10 cal, 14 x 6 pounder, 6 x 1 pounder and four colts, and originally six torpedo tubes. Her armour is 4.75" on the deck, 2" on the deck ends, 4" on barbettes and turrets, 4"–5" on sponsons and 5" C. Ts fore and aft. Her machinery consisted of two sets of vertical triple expansion engines, with two screws. Boilers were cylindrical, 4 x 2 ended and 2 x 1 ended and she had ten furnaces. Her designed SHP was 17,000 = twenty-one knots and she was coal-fired, normally carrying 500 tonnes but the maximum could be 1,300 tonnes. Her signal letter was 'N'. She was partially reconstructed in 1900 to 1903. Her total cost was approximately $41.5 million, a vast sum in those days.

Her first role was as flagship of Admiral Dewey in the Asiatic squadron and she first saw action on the morning of 1st May 1989 when she led a column of cruisers and gunboats into Manila Bay and was the first ship to open fire that day. All ten ships of the Spanish squadron were destroyed by the US squadron led by *Olympia*. After her overhaul in 1903, she was re-commissioned and was then assigned to the North Atlantic squadron for four years and then was relegated to be a training ship, then to a barracks ship, and finally to the reserve. She was brought out of retirement in the First World War and went on patrol duties in the North Atlantic and Mediterranean. She was finally de-commissioned on 1st September 1922 and whilst in reserve was allowed to badly deteriorate until 1954, when it was decided by the City of Philadelphia to try to obtain her for preservation. She was finally purchased in 1957 and transferred to The Cruiser Olympia Association. She now lies, well preserved, at Philadelphia's Penn's Landing in her final mooring place, a monument and testament to the City in their courage and foresight to buy and preserve such a wonderful piece of history. They must be congratulated as all those concerned in preservation of these ships should be. The proudest moment in her career was when she brought home to America the body of their Unknown Warrior from France to be interred in Arlington cemetery.

23

Plate 23 – USS Olympia *(Photo courtesy of Cruiser* Olympia *Association). Also enshrined is USS* Becuna *(see Page 36).*

Plate 24 – USS Olympia *and USS* Becuna *(Photo courtesy of Cruiser* Olympia *Association).*

24

USS *YORKTOWN* (CV10)

This Second World War aircraft carrier is also of the Essex class of twenty-four ships (as is *Hornet* CV12). She was laid down at Newport News on 1st December 1941.

Launched on 21st January 1943 and completed and commissioned on 4th April 1943, she was originally to be named *Bon Homme Richard* but her name was changed before launching. Her statistics are the same as USS *Hornet*, a sister ship. The previous ship of this name was CV5, which was lost during the battle of Midway in June 1942. This ship was in the thick of action and her guns shot down fourteen enemy aircraft whilst her pilots shot down 458 and destroyed 695 on the ground. These operations earned her the Presidential Unit Citation and also fifteen battle stars and other awards for operations in the Pacific. She fought in many historic battles against the Japanese and served at Truk, The Marianas, Philippines, Iwo Jima and Okinawa. She also served off Korea and also during the War in Vietnam. She had the distinction, like *Hornet*, of recovering the crew of the *Apollo Eight* mission in 1968. She was de-commissioned on 9th January 1947 and was put into the reserve fleet until she was re-commissioned on 15th December 1952 for duty in the Korean War. There she earned further honours, namely the Korean Service Medal and the United Nations Medal and, later, in the Vietnam conflict, she earned the Armed Forces Expeditionary Medal and the Vietnam Service Medal. The *Yorktown* was finally de-commissioned in 1970, towed from New Jersey to Charleston in 1975, and was acquired by the Patriots Point Development Authority in 1975 where she has been ever since. She held the distinction at that time of being the only aircraft carrier to be preserved in the world, a record that is now obsolete with the other carriers that are preserved, but still a good record to hold then.

Also in this class were *Intrepid* (CV11) (Page 27) and *Hornet* (CV12) (Page 23).

Technical specifications:

Of 27,100 tonnes (33,000 full load) she is 888ft long overall, has a hull beam of 93ft and a width of 147ft, and draught of 30ft. She carried 12 x 5" guns, 44–72 40mm AA, 52 x 20mm in quad. mounts. She carried up to ninety aircraft. Her armour is 3" x 2ft side amidships, 3" on hangar deck, 1.5 on flight deck and 1.5" on upper deck. Machinery: geared turbines, four shafts. SHP 150,000 = thirty-three knots. Boilers are eight Babcock & Wilcox. Her complement was 380 officers and 3,088 men (wartime).

In the 1950s she was modified with the addition of an angled flight deck, which increased her tonnage to 41,000 tonnes, and then she was converted into an anti-submarine carrier. It was in this capacity that she served in the Vietnam War.

Contact details:

USS *Yorktown*, Patriot's Point Development Authority, PO Box 986, Mt Pleasant, South Carolina, 29664, USA.

Plate 25 – USS Yorktown *(Photo courtesy of Patriot's Point Development Authority).*
Plate 26 – USS Yorktown *(Photo courtesy of Patriot's Point Development Authority).*

USS *HORNET* (CV12)

This *Hornet* is the eighth ship to bear this illustrious name; the first was a sailing ship launched in 1775, a sloop of ten guns which fought in the Revolutionary War, and the second fought the Barbary pirates in 1805 and assisted the Marines at Derne. There were a further four ships of the name, then came the famous *Hornet* (CV8) that launched Doolittle's bombers to raid Japan and give them one hell of a shock. She was only in commission for a year, took part in three battles that broke the back of the Japanese campaign, but was sunk in October 1942. This ship was commissioned on 29th November 1943 and was the fourth ship of twenty-four Essex class ships, of which fourteen were cancelled.

Technical specifications:

Her length is 888ft overall, beam 93ft, draught 29ft. Maximum displacement was 27,100 tonnes (war) with a crew of 3,500. Machinery by Newport News (builders). Geared turbines x four shafts. SHP = thirty-three knots. Laid down in 1942, she carried 12 x 5" guns, 72 x 40mm and 52 x 20mm in quad mounts. She carried 100+ planes and 4" armour over machinery spaces.

She served well in the Second World War and earned a Presidential Unit Citation and nine battle stars. During fourteen months of her war career she never tied up to a pier. That's busy! Her planes destroyed 1,400 enemy planes and sunk seventy-three ships. A record. She was attacked fifty-nine times but never suffered a major hit and she was in the Vietnam War and was deployed three times to Southeast Asia in that time. Her most notable feat was the recovery of the *Apollo Eleven* space capsule with Neil Armstrong and Buzz Aldrin from their moon walk. She then recovered *Apollo Twelve* four months later with all its Navy crew. In 1950 she was modernised and made into attack carrier *CV12*, but was later reassigned as an anti-submarine carrier *CVS12*.

Finally she was retired from service and put into reserve on 26th June 1970 and was put with the mothballed fleet at Bremerton, Washington for twenty-five years. In 1995 she was sold to a scrap metal company and taken to San Francisco area to be scrapped. Towed to Alamanda Air Station for the 50th anniversary of the end of the Second World War in May 1995, the Aircraft Carrier Hornet Foundation was formed and in November 1995 the Navy put her in The Ship Donation Programme, which gave the ACHF time to raise funds to buy her. In September 1997 they had raised $2.1 million in donations and loans and the *Hornet* was transferred in 1998. About 200 hard-working staff and volunteers worked to recondition her and prepare her for public exhibition, and they are to be congratulated for their zeal, hard work and dedication. A job well done! She's now located at Alamanda Point, CA. She was opened for public viewing on 27th August

1998, but was formally opened by the moon walker, Dr Buzz Aldrin, who was guest of honour and the featured main speaker in October 1998. She is now a popular venue and she receives many thousands of visitors, who not only enjoy going over her, but can stay overnight as do many children and some groups who also use her as a meeting place. She is well worth the effort to see and is well preserved; in fact a really good day's outing. Please try to support her if possible, to help maintain her in the pristine and beautiful condition that they have restored her to.

Contact details:

Aircraft Carrier *Hornet* Museum. 707 W Hornet Ave, Pier 3, Alamanda Point. CA 94501, USA.
Telephone: 510 521 8448, Fax: 510 521 8327.
Website: www.usshornet.org and www.hornetevents.com

Plate 27 – USS Hornet *brochure. (Photo courtesy of Aircraft Carrier* Hornet *Museum with many thanks for their assistance).*
Plate 28 – Map of California.
Plate 29 – USS Hornet *(Photos courtesy of Aircraft Carrier* Hornet *Museum with many thanks for their assistance).*

USS *MIDWAY* (CV41)

USS *Midway* is the name ship of a class of six ships but three were cancelled in 1945. She was ordered on 7th August 1942, and her keel was laid down on 27th October 1943. Launched on 20th March 1945 she was commissioned on 11th September 1945. Built by Newport News Co., she was the first of the fleet carriers to be named after a Second World War battle and the third ship and second carrier to bear this name. The first had her name changed to USS *Panay* in 1943 and the second, a carrier of the small Casablanca class, was changed from *Chapin Bay* to *Midway* and then to *St Lo* (CVE 63). It was lost on 25th October 1944.

Technical specifications:

Midway's displacement was (war load) 55,000 tonnes with a length overall of 986ft, beam of 136ft and draught of 32.75ft. Four shaft geared turbines, SHP = 20,000 = thirty-three knots. Twelve Babcock & Wilcox boilers. Crew from 3,000 to 4,085 men. She had heavy armour and carried 137 aircraft (including large bombers), 18 x 5" 54 cal guns, 84 x 40mm AA (Quads), 82 x 20mm AA but now has 14 x 5", and 21 Quads. She cost $90 million.

She was commissioned too late for the Second World War but spent much of her time at sea, notably Atlantic, Pacific and Caribbean areas, and was in the Korean and Vietnam Wars. De-commissioned for the first time in October 1955, she underwent a refit when the British inventions of steam catapults and angled flight decks were added to her, thus increasing her weight to total 62,000 tonnes. She then had another overhaul in October 1962 to April 1963. In February 1966 she was again de-commissioned and had a four-year refit, costing $202 million. On 20th June 1990 she had two bad explosions on board with a fire that burned for ten hours with three dead and eight injured. She arrived at North Island, San Diego on 14th September 1991 but went to sea again on 24th September for some evaluation trials. She was finally de-commissioned on 11th April 1992 and struck from the Navy List on 17th March 1997, and then stored at Bremerton, Washington. On 30th September 2003, she was again underway, but this time being towed by tugs to Oakland, California. She arrived on 7th October 2003 and after some restoration work was done on her, she was then again under tow to North Island and then to her final resting place at Navy Pier, San Diego. She was opened to the public on 7th June 2004 and has since never looked back. I visited her in early 2007 and as an ex-Royal Navy and carrier man, I found her to be huge compared with the carrier that I served on. She is a magnificent showpiece, very well preserved and lovingly cared for by 'her' people and well worth the while to go and visit her and her many aircraft exhibits. Her motto was 'Midway Magic'. She held the distinction of being the longest serving carrier in the US Navy, a proud total of forty-seven years' service.

For full details of her history go to www.midway.org

30

31

Plate 30 –
USS Midway
(Author's
collection).
Plate 31 –
USS Midway
(Author's
collection).

USS *INTREPID* (CV11)

The *Intrepid* is a sister ship to USS *Hornet* (*CV12*. Page 23) and *Yorktown* (*CV10*. Page 21) so her details are similar in most respects. Two other ships of this class were cancelled in 1945, *The Reprisal* and *The Iwo Jima* (ex Crown Point). *Intrepid*'s keel was laid down on 1st December 1941 and she was completed on 16th August 1943. She went straight off to War and was in the thick of it at Kwajalun and Truk where she was torpedoed, and after repairs she then went to Palau, Leyte Gulf and was then struck by a kamikaze off Luzon on 25th November 1944. Repaired again, she then was struck by another kamikaze at Okinawa on 16th April 1945. She finally saw the War out and saw duty in the Atlantic and the Mediterranean and in the early 1960s she served as a recovery ship for space flights. After doing three more tours of duty, she was put on the Reserve and then was de-commissioned and turned over to The Intrepid Museum Foundation, which opened The Intrepid Sea Air Space Museum on 3rd August 1982. She is moored in the main harbour in New York on the Circle Line Pier and, like her sister ships, is well worth a visit with all her impressive displays of aircraft and space memorabilia.

32

Plate 32 – USS Intrepid *in New York Harbour (Author's collection).*

33

Plate 33 – USS Intrepid *in New York Harbour (Author's collection).*

USS *JOSEPH P KENNEDY JR.* (DD850)

This destroyer is of the Gearing class, which were a modified type of the Sumner class (see *Laffey DD724*) and they had 14ft extra built in amidships. She was laid down on 26th July 1945 and therefore was built too late to see any Second World War action.

Technical specifications:

She displaced 2,425 tonnes (3,300 tonnes war load). Her length is 390.5ft overall x 40.75ft x 19ft draught. Her machinery is by her builders who were Bethlehem Steel Corp, Quincy, Mass. and comprises of two shafts with geared turbines, SHP 60,000 = thirty-five knots. Four Babcock & Wilcox boilers. Armament 6 x 5" (3 x 2), 12 x 40 MM AA, 4 x 20mm AA, with 10 x 21" TTs and a crew of 350. She saw action in Korea and Vietnam but was eventually put into reserve and then sold to her present owners who have restored her and she is now on display with USS *Lionfish* and USS *Massachusetts*. (See Page 12.)

Also preserved is the same class of sister ship, USS *Orleck DD 886,* which is now preserved at Orange in Texas. 105 ships were built in this class of ship.

USS *LAFFEY* (DD724)

This destroyer, which is of the Allen M Sumner class, is one of fifty-eight ships built during the Second World War, of which there were five war losses, and this class were an improved Gearing class ship. She was launched on 21st November 1943 and is the second ship to bear this name. The first ship was also a destroyer and was named after a seaman, Barlett Laffey, who was a Civil War Medal of Honour recipient. She was built at Bethlehem Iron Works at Maine and commissioned on 8th February 1944.

Technical specifications:

Length 376.5ft overall x 40.10ft beam x draught of 19ft. Displacement (war load) of 3,000 tonnes. Her guns were 6 x 5" x 38cal, 12 x 40mm AA, 11 x 20mm AA and 6 DCTs. 5 x 21" TTs. She has Geared Turbines by the builders x two shafts, SHP 60,000 = thirty-four knots. Four Babcock & Wilcox boilers and carried a wartime crew of 350 men. She cost $8 million. Her first war action was at Normandy, France in 1944 where she bombarded the beaches before the troops landed. At the end of the War in Europe, she was transferred to the Pacific theatre of war, where she served in the Philippines and then went to Iwo Jima and Okinawa, where she was attacked by twenty-two kamikaze planes whilst escorting the carrier *Yorktown* and was hit by six planes and had three bomb hits to her in April 1945 but she still fought on, although she had thirty-two men killed and seventy-one wounded, but she gallantly shot down eleven of her attackers and stayed afloat to safely reach home port and be repaired for further service to her country. She was present at the 1946 Bikini Atoll Atom Bomb tests of 1946 and also present in Korean waters during that war. She then operated in the North Atlantic and the Mediterranean and then after such a proud service she was finally de-commissioned in 1975 and laid up in Reserve until 1981, when she was purchased and then towed to Patriot's Point to be prepared as a museum ship, where she now lies with the other two ships that are located and preserved there. See Plate 21 on Page 22.

Contact details:

Address is the same as USS *Yorktown*.

USS *STEWART* (DE238)

This Escort destroyer of the Edsall class was laid down on 22nd November 1942 at Brown's shipbuilding Yard (Houston) Texas. She took the name of a previous ship (DD224) which was lost on 2nd March 1942, salvaged by the Japanese and then recovered in August 1945, finally being sunk as a target on 24th May 1946.

Technical specifications:

Of 1,200 tonnes, she is 306ft overall x 36.75ft beam x 8.75ft draught, with two shaft geared turbines. SHP 6,000 = twenty-one knots. Armament was 3 x 3", 8 x 40mm AA and 3 x 21" TT, carrying a crew of 200 men. At the end of the Second World War, she was paid off with many of her sister ships and put into Reserve and was eventually bought by the City of Galveston, where she is now on exhibition with the submarine USS *Cavalla* (SS244). See Plate 36 on Page 32.

Contact details:

Sea Wolf Park, PO Box 3306, Galveston, Texas, 77550, USA.

Plate 34 – USS Stewart *DE238.*
(Photo courtesy of City of Galveston.)

GATO CLASS SUBMARINES

Six of the submarines that are preserved in the USA are of the Gato class.

Technical specifications:

Displacement of 1,525 tonnes (2,415 at war load). Dimensions 311.75ft long x 27.3ft beam x 15.3ft draught. Two shaft diesels, BHP 5,400 = twenty knots. Electric motors BHP 2,740 = ten knots. 10 x 21" Torpedo Tubes (six bow and four stern). 1 x 5' 1 x 40mm guns. Crew of eighty men. Built from 1941 onwards, they saw sterling service and are listed as follows and where located. Nineteen of this class were lost with all hands.

USS *SILVERSIDES* (SS-236)

The *Silversides* was built by Mare Island N. Yard and was launched on 26th August 1941. On trials, during a quick dive, her stern planes jammed and she hit the bottom and during her first sea patrol her radioman was stuck on the conning tower as she was diving, but, luckily for him, his cries of distress were heard. On 10th May 1942 she engaged a Japanese trawler and was raked by machine gun fire, which killed the second loader on the gun with a shot into the temple. However, she sank the trawler. On 17th May she sank a 4,000 tonne Japanese merchant man. During Christmas week of 1942, an appendectomy was carried out on a crewman, the third ever to be performed on a submarine. On 4th June 1943 she laid a minefield in Steffen Strait, between New Hanover and New Ireland. During her wartime career, she sank twenty-three ships with a total of 90,080 tonnes, one of the highest tallies.

She is the holder of four Presidential Unit Citations and twelve combat insignia stars. She is credited with one of the most superbly executed attacks of the War. She fired six torpedoes for five hits and three sinkings. Attacking a Japanese convoy on 18th January 1943, she sank the *Surabaya Maru, Sonedone Maru* and *Mieu Maru.* Following the end of the Second World War she was towed up the Mississippi River to Chicago where she served for twenty-three years as a Naval Reserve training boat.

De-commissioned in 1969, she lay idle until 1973, when she was presented to The Combined Great Lakes Navy Association, who have restored her to her original condition for public display.

Contact details:

The Combined Great Lakes Navy Association Inc., 3227 Central St, Evanston, Illinois, 60201, USA.

Plate 35 – USS Silverside *(Photo courtesy of The Combined Great Lakes Navy Association Inc.).*

USS CAVALLA (SS-244)

The *Cavalla* was built by the Electric Boat Co., and launched on 14th November 1943. She went straight into war service. She was involved in the campaign in the Marianas with a group of nine submarines where she was stationed in the westward area. On her maiden patrol, on 18th June, she sank the Japanese carrier *Shokaku* of 30,000 tonnes, a notable feat indeed. She was present with eleven other submarines when the Japanese signed the Instrument of Surrender onboard *Missouri* (see Page 3).

She was finally paid off to the Reserve Fleet and then deleted from the Navy List and put up for disposal. She was bought by the City of Galveston and put into the care of the Park Board of Trustees who has well preserved her and she can be seen at Galveston where she is moored to be visited and admired for her sterling service.

<u>Contact details:</u>

Sea Wolf Park, PO Box 3306, Galveston, Texas, 77550, USA.

Plate 36 – USS Cavalla
*(Photo courtesy of The Park
Board of Trustees, City of
Galveston).*

USS *COBIA* (SS245)

The *Cobia* is also of the Gato class of submarines, and was also built by the Electric
Boat Co., and launched on 28th November 1943. She saw good war service and in
December 1962 she was re-designated AGSS. Finally paid off, she was purchased by
the City of Manitowoc for preservation and after an overhaul she has been put on view
for visitors at the Manitowoc Maritime Museum. She is very well maintained and in
pristine condition and well worth a visit.

Plate 37 – USS Cobia
*SS245. (Photo courtesy
of Manitowoc Maritime
Museum.)*

USS *COD* (SS224)

The *Cod* of the Gato class was built by the Electric Boat Co., and launched on 21st
March 1943, and was based at Fremantle in Western Australia where she sallied forth
to fight against the Japanese aggressors and did most of her war service in the Manila
area, plus the Pacific. She was put on to AGSS, with many of her sisters, in December
1962. She was put up for disposal at the end of her service. She was purchased by the
State of Ohio and is now on display at Cleveland, Ohio.

USS *CROAKER* (SS246)

The *Croaker*, like many of her sister boats, was built by the Electric Boat Co., and was launched on 19th December 1943. She did good war service and in August 1951 was re-designated as SSK and then AGSS in June 1963. Finally she was put up for sale, was purchased and put up for display and for visiting at Groton in Connecticut where she can now be seen.

USS *DRUM* (SS228)

The *Drum* was built in Portsmouth Navy Dockyard and was launched on 12th May 1941. During her war service, she sank a total of fifteen ships with a tonnage of 80,580 tonnes, a good record. She was re-designated to AGSS in December 1962 and finally paid off into Reserve and then put up for disposal. She was then bought by the City of Alabama and put on display with the USS *Alabama* at Battleship Park where she can be visited, along with the battleship. (See Plate 16 on Page 14.)

BALAO *CLASS*

The Balao class of submarines were an upgraded version of the Gato class and were built from 1943 to 1945 (although one, the *Tiru*, was not finished until 1947).

Technical specifications:

Their displacement was of 1,526 tonnes and their dimensions were 311.75 x 27.2 x 13.74ft. Guns were 1 x 3" x 50 cal 2 x 20mm AA (some had 1 x 5"). 10 x 21" tubes, six bow, four stern. Their machinery was GM Fairbanks Morse or HOR diesels. BHP 6,500 = twenty-one knots. War losses were eleven boats, one of which was by its own torpedo, and at War's end many were sold off to Canada, Turkey, Holland, Spain, Venezuela, Italy, Brazil, Greece, Chile and Argentina (one of which, the *Santa Fey*, ex-*Lamprey*, was sunk by the British forces at the Falklands conflict). Five were sunk as target ships, three of them at the Bikini Atoll Atomic tests. A total of 122 of this class were built and were a most successful type of submarine with many 'kills' to their credits.

USS *GLAGAMORE* (SS343)

This submarine, which is of the numerous wartime Balao class of 122 boats, is also moored at Patriot's Point with *Yorktown* and *Laffey,* whom she lies beside. Built by the Electric Boat Co., New London, Conn., she was launched on 23rd February 1945 and commissioned in June 1945 just before the end of the Second World War. She spent thirty years of Naval service on general duties and was rebuilt and then modified into a Guppy class of submarine. She was finally de-commissioned in the city of Philadelphia in 1975 and then taken under tow to Patriot's Point in 1981 where she now lies, open for viewing with the other ships there. (See Pages 21–22)

USS *LING* (SS297)

This boat of the Balao class was built at Cramp's yard and launched on 15th August 1943 and saw active service, but only did one patrol before the end of the Second World War. In December 1962 she then became AGSS and when retired from the Navy List she was donated to the Submarine Memorial Association of Hackensack, NJ, and she now lies at the wharf in Borg Park on display to be visited.

Ling was commissioned on 8th June 1945 and made only one patrol before War's end. De-commissioned on 26th October 1946, she joined the New London Group, Atlantic Reserve Fleet, and was reactivated as a training ship in 1960, and in 1962 she was at New York as a Naval Reservist's ship. Again de-commissioned in December 1967, she was then struck from the Navy list in December 1971. She was then donated to the Submarine Memorial Association. She arrived at her present location on 13th January 1973.

Contact details:
PO Box 395, Hackensack, NJ, 07602, USA.

Plate 38 – USS Ling *(Photo courtesy of Hackensack Submarine Memorial Association).*

USS *BOWFIN* (SS287)

The *Bowfin* was built at Portsmouth New York Yard and launched on 7th December 1942. During her war career she sank sixteen ships with a total tonnage of 67,882. In September 1943, she was on her maiden voyage in the South China Sea when she encountered the passenger cargoman, *Kirishma Maru* of 8,120 tonnes, and promptly sunk her. Two days later she met with an enemy convoy and fired three torpedoes at a Japanese tanker. One struck the bow and another hit amidships and the tanker caught fire and then *Bowfin* sank another ship in the convoy. She then headed towards Cape Varella to find the rest of the convoy and blew an 8,000 tonne ship to pieces with four torpedoes. The next day she met and sunk a small coastal steamer with three torpedoes. She received a report from *Billfish* already operating in the area, of five ships in a convoy; she sank the leading ship, and the second ship. The third ship turned and attacked *Bowfin* with gunfire, scoring a hit on the conning tower, which caused some damage but *Bowfin* fired from the stern tubes and sank this ship also. On the way home, she sank a seventy-five tonne oil-carrying yacht and headed for her home port of Fremantle in West Australia, arriving on 9th December 1943. She saw more war service and in December 1962 she was AGSS. Finally she was released from the Navy List and purchased for preservation, arriving at Pearl Harbour where she is now on view and open for visitors alongside the Submarine Memorial Park there.

39

Plate 39 – USS Bowfin *(Author's collection).*
Plate 40 –USS Bowfin *at* Hawaii *(Author's collection).*
Plate 41 – USS Bowfin *at* Hawaii *(Author's collection).*

USS *CABRILLA* (SS288)

This boat was built at Portsmouth Navy Yard and launched on 24th December 1942. She served several war patrols and one of her notable forays against the Japanese was on 20th October 1943, when, at Negros, she took aboard a Major Villamor and four other men, which resulted in a clandestine landing to help arrange the Philippine guerrilla movement.

After the War, like many of this class of submarine, she became AGSS in December 1962 and eventually was released from the Navy List to be put up for disposal. She was then sold to Battleship Texas Commission and now rests on display and for viewing with that battleship at San Jacinto State Park.

USS *LIONFISH* (SS298)

This boat was built by Cramp Boatyard and launched on 7th November 1943. She served several war patrols and in December 1962 she was also AGSS, finally being put in Reserve and then sold off to the USS Massachusetts Memorial Committee Inc., for her preservation where she now lies with the battleship (see Plate 14 on Page 12).

USS *BECUNA* (SS319)

Built by the Electric Boat Co., *Becuna* was launched on 30th January 1944 and served in the Pacific and also the Philippines areas and was sold to The Cruiser Olympia Association where she is now on display and open to visitors at Philadelphia's Penn Landing. (see Plate 23 on Page 20.)

USS *PAMPANITO* (SS383)

This boat was built at the Portsmouth Navy yard, New Hampshire, and launched on 12th July 1943. She served six patrols and sank 27,000 tonnes of enemy ships, and also had the proud distinction of saving seventy-three ex-POWs sunk on *Kachidoki Maru*. At War's end she became a training ship and was de-commissioned on 15th December 1945. She was finally sold to the National Maritime Museum Association on 20th May 1976 for display at Pier 45, Fisherman's Wharf, San Francisco.

She was used in the film 'Down Periscope'.

Contact details:

National Maritime Museum Association, PO Box 470310, San Francisco, CA, 947147-0310, USA

Website: http://www.maritime.org/pamphone.shtml.

Plate 42 – USS Pampanito *(Author's collection).*

Plate 43 – USS Pampanito *(Author's collection).*

USS *BATFISH* (SS310)

Batfish was originally laid down as USS *Acoupa* but was renamed before her launch on 5th May 1943 at Portsmouth, New Hampshire. Total tonnage sunk by her was 37,080 plus three enemy subs – nine Battle Stars. She served mainly in the Pacific area but in October 1944 she was part of a force that was awaiting a Japanese force off Formosa, which was threatening the army landings on the Philippines. She was then stationed on the Sulu Sea off Northwest Mindanao. At War's end, she was relegated for training purposes and then to AGSS in December 1962 and finally to the Reserve fleet from where she was put up to disposal and then bought by the City of Muskogee, where she is now lying and open for visitors. Her awards for heroism were one Navy Cross, four Silver Stars and ten Bronze Stars.

Batfish (SS310) set the record for US submarines sinking enemy submarines during the Second World War. She also had the unique experience of being the first US submarine on which a divine service was held whilst submerged in a war zone. This aggressive submarine compiled her record during the years between 1944 and 1945 when Japanese shipping was hard to find. *Batfish* ended the War with a record of fourteen vessels sunk and three damaged, for a total of 37,080 tonnes of enemy shipping sunk. On her first war patrol, on the night of 19th January 1944, she made a torpedo attack on a convoy of four Japanese ships and hit two large freighters and sank *Hidaku Maru*. On her third patrol, six attacks were made, the first one on 10th June 1944, when she attacked a large freighter with three torpedoes, and the enemy ship literally 'blew up' and sank in less than two minutes, going down by the stern. Shortly after noon on 18th June a small cargo ship and a tanker were sighted and *Batfish* fired three torpedoes, one of which hit the cargo ship which broke in half and sank. At 12:38 on 22nd June, *Batfish* fired four torpedoes at another Japanese ship and scored hits forward and aft and the ship sank rapidly. She was depth charged with altogether fifty-one charges but received no damage. At 10:20 on 29th June she sighted a Japanese trawler escorted by a yacht-type patrol boat and the Captain decided upon a surface action. The four inch gun scored ten hits which started fires, and then she engaged the escort who was trying to sneak up on her, and at 12:15 it stopped and started to sink after numerous hits. At 18:35 the following day, she departed for Midway and arrived on 7th July at the submarine base there. She underwent a refit and minor repairs until 31st July 1944. On 31st July she sailed on her fourth patrol and discovered a destroyer aground on Verlasco Reef, and she fired three torpedoes and all scored hits, which left the destroyer smoking heavily and sinking fast. At 18:31 on 26th August, she fired a spread of torpedoes at a Fubuki class destroyer and they sheared the stern off her and the no. two funnel fell over. On 3rd September she headed for Fremantle, Australia and arrived on 12th September. She sank another small cargo ship on 11th November in San Fernando Harbour. On 14th November, in company with the US submarines *Ray* and *Ralton*, they attacked a convoy and *Batfish* fired her four stern tubes at a medium-sized cargo ship, which blew up and sank. On 2nd February, on her sixth patrol, she went into the Luzon Straits and there sunk a large landing craft. On 9th February 1945 she sighted a Japanese T class submarine and her second torpedo hit the sub, and it exploded violently and sank. On 11th February she sighted another enemy submarine, which she tracked until it submerged. *Batfish* waited and at 22:02 it resurfaced and *Batfish* fired torpedoes and the submarine exploded and the second torpedo hit the sinking sub on the conning tower. At 03:00 on 13th February, yet another sub contact was made and three stern tubes were fired. At 04:49, the first torpedo hit and the target sank at once. This target was seen literally to blow apart in a ball of yellow flame and fire. On her seventh patrol, she shelled the village of Nagata and set it all on fire. On 9th August, she sank a mine with her 20mm guns. On 26th August, she arrived back at Pearl Harbour and then proceeded to San Francisco where she underwent preservation processing prior to de-commissioning.

Contact details:

USS *Batfish*, Muskogee War Memorial Park, PO Box 253, Muskogee, Oklahoma 74401, USA.
Telephone: (918) 682 6294. Open hours: Weekdays 9 a.m. – 5 p.m., Sundays 12 noon – 6 p.m. Open: 15th March – 15th October.

Plate 44 *– USS* Batfish. *Photo courtesy of Muskogee War Memorial Park, Muskogee, Oklahoma, USA.*

EXPLORER

Though not officially a warship, the *Explorer* deserves a mention as a forerunner of submarines. She was completed in 1932, at twenty-two feet long, six feet wide and weighing 20,000 pounds. Electric motors could drive either the propeller or the wheels. She could move sideways as well as forward. She carried two crew members and two passengers, with a diver's escape hatch from the bottom and portholes for viewings, lights for visibility, stirrers for removal of silt and a mechanical arm for retrieving items. She has been preserved and restored by Submarine Support Facility 101.

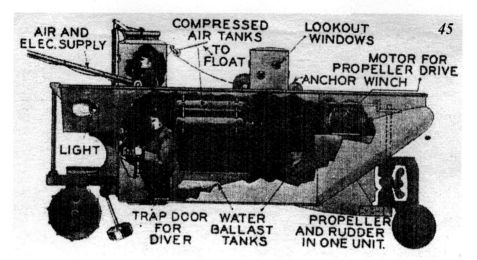

Plate 45 – The Explorer. *(Photo courtesy of Submarine Support Facility.)*

U-505

This Kreigsmarine submarine is on dry land outside the Museum of Science and Industry at Chicago where she was brought overland from Michigan. A Type IXC, she was built by Deutsche Werft of Hamburg, and was launched on 24th May 1941.

Technical specifications:

She displaced 1,120 / 1,232 tonnes, is 252 x 22.25 x 15.5ft with two shaft diesel electric motors. She carried 208 tonnes of fuel with a range of approximately 11,000 miles. She had 1 x 4.1" gun (later removed), 1 x 37mm AA, 1 x 20mm, 6 x 21" tubes (four forward and two aft). Complement of forty-eight men and Schnorchel added later.

On 4th June 1944 she was depth-charged by USN aircraft carrier *Guadalcanal* (CVE60) and escort destroyers *Chatelain* (DE149), *Jenks* (DE665), *Pillsbury* (DE133), *Flaherty* (DE135) and *Pope* (DE665) NW of Dakar and captured. She was re-named USN *Nemo* in 1944, but never used by the US Navy, and was removed to Chicago as a Naval relic.

Plate 46 – *Bow on view of* U-505 *in place before the Museum of Science and Industry in Chicago. (Photo courtesy of Chicago Museum.)*

Plate 47 – *A tow line is secured to the U-505 (type ISC) after she had surrendered to a US Navy escort group comprising the escort carrier* Guadalcanal *and three destroyer escorts. She was then towed 2,500 miles to Bermuda (left) I.W.M.*

PIONEER

A Confederate Privateer Submarine located at Presbytere Arcade in Louisiana State Museum. She was scuttled in 1861 and raised from the seabed to be preserved and put on display.

Plate 48 – Pioneer *(Photo courtesy of Louisiana State Museum).*

JAPANESE TWO-MAN SUBMARINE – MATO No: 8

This submarine at the Submarine Base Museum was salvaged intact off Cape Esperance, Guadalcanal by USS *Ortolan* (Lt. Cdr. A. D. Holland commanding) during the period between 24th April and 6th June 1943 by Cdr. F. X. Sommer (MC) USNR, the diving officer. She was then towed to Espiritu Santo and put aboard SS *Passiac* to be shipped to the United States.

Technical specifications:

Hull 70–80 tonnes, length 74'3", overall length 80'6", hull of ¼ plate, carried 2 x 18" torpedoes and 1 x 200 lb demolition charge.

Japanese two-man submarines at Naval Submarine Base, New London, Groton, Conn. One (Plate 49) is a cutaway used for training purposes and the other (Plate 50) was recovered off Cape Esperance. Also at the base is the Type Seehund II (Seahound) HU75 from the German Kreigsmarine (Plate 51). Another can be found at The Navy Yard, Washington. All three Plates are courtesy of the New London Submarine Base. Also at this base is a 'Maiale' Italian two-man submarine, used at Alexandria, Egypt, when they badly damaged HM ships *Queen Elizabeth* and *Valiant*. At the Mariner's Museum, Newport News, can be found a German one-man torpedo-carrying 'Marder' type submarine.

Plate 49 *– Japanese two-man submarine – a cutaway used for training purposes. (Photo courtesy of the New London Submarine Base.)*

Plate 50 *– Japanese two-man submarine – recovered off Cape Esperance. (Photo courtesy of the New London Submarine Base.)*

GERMAN SUBMARINE TYPE II
SEEHUND (HU 75)

In 1945, after the cessation of hostilities with Germany, this midget submarine was shipped from Germany to Batonne, NJ. In May 1946 and after some tests were carried out on her, *Hu 75* was turned over to the Submarine Base for display. This submarine, of which Germany had many, was carried by trailer along the French coast for launching at any strategic point. The torpedoes were carried outside of the hull and were fired from this position inside.

Plate 51 – *Type* Seehund II *(*Seahound*) HU75. (Photo courtesy of the New London Submarine Base.)*

Plate 52 – *German submarine with a deckload of midget subs (1945). (Captured German Photograph.)*

Plate 53 – Seehund. *In the process of assembly at a gigantic shelter where individual sections were delivered. (Photo courtesy of Imperial War Museum).*

Plate 54 – Seehund. *Lying at anchor after being in action. (Photo courtesy of Imperial War Museum.)*

KAITEN

This is a Japanese one-man suicide Torpedo, first used in 1944. 'Kaiten' means to make a reverse in the course of events. The Japanese hoped that this new weapon would do that in the Pacific. This was a torpedo with a small cockpit, periscope and manual controls for steering speed and depth. It had a pure oxygen, kerosene-burning 550 HP engine with a 3,000 lb warhead on it. They were taken by a 'Mother' sub, to within five miles of the target and then released. The upper hatch was to be used to escape from but was never believed to have been used. Ninety-six Kaiten pilots died (sixteen in training). This exhibit can be seen at the museum at Pearl Harbour.

Plates 55 and 56 – Kaiten *(Photos courtesy of author's collection).*

SS JEREMIAH O'BRIEN

Whilst this ship is not a warship, I must admit that I feel she should be included as the sole representative left of a class of ships that help beat the U-Boats and were built for war purposes, so I have taken the step to include her as a tribute to this class of ship and their contribution to Victory. The ships that follow are of the British 'Ocean' class of tramp steamers, the first built of which was the *'Empire Liberty'* from which came the name of the 'Liberty' boats. The first Liberty ship to be built was the *Patrick Henry* on 27th September 1941 (and President Roosevelt's statement that they were 'Ugly Ducklings' stuck to them and this was their nickname). This was the first of 2,710 ships to be built to this design. Many, after War's end, went on for years in civilian use, and the last was scrapped in 1987, forty-four years later than when they were thought to be finished with. *Jeremiah O'Brien* was launched on 19th June 1943 by the New England Shipbuilding Corp., at Portland and built in fifty-six days, and named after the first US Naval hero of the Revolutionary War. She was a steam boat, coal-fired and capable of eleven knots. Under the management of Grace Lines, she carried war supplies across the Atlantic and from June 1944 ferried troops and material to the Normandy beach-heads.

From July 1943 to October 1944, she made four voyages between the USA and Britain as part of convoys. On her fourth voyage she was diverted to run supplies to the American D-Day beaches at Normandy. She completed eleven trips before returning to the USA and she was the target of two bomb attacks and one torpedo attack by submarine, but it missed. Her fifth voyage in October 1944 went from New York, through the Panama Canal to Chile and Peru, then returning to New Orleans. Her sixth was a trip to the Philippines and then back to San Francisco. Her final seventh voyage was from July 1945 to January 1946. She sailed from San Francisco to Australia, Calcutta, Shanghai, Manila and then back to San Francisco. On her return journey she carried eleven Australian war brides to the US to join their American husbands there. Her eleven shuttle voyages ferrying troops and supplies to the Normandy beach-heads were as follows.

Ports of call: New York, New York; Brooklyn, New York; Gourock, Scotland; Southampton, England.

1. Omaha Beach-head, Normandy / Southampton, England.
2. Omaha beach-head / Southampton / Belfast, Northern Ireland.
3. Utah beach-head, Normandy / Southampton.
4. Utah beach-head / Southampton.
5. Omaha beach-head / Southampton.
6. Omaha beach-head / Southampton.
7. Utah beach-head / Southampton.
8. Utah beach-head / Southampton.
9. Utah beach-head / Southampton.
10. Utah beach-head / Southampton.
11 Utah beach-head / Cherbourg, France. Mumbles Point, Swansea, Wales. Milford Haven, England. New York, New York.

In February 1946, she was laid up in reserve at Suisun Bay, Cal., and stayed there for thirty-three years. In 1966, the need for a Liberty ship memorial was perceived and in

1978, she was then selected and the Liberty Ship Memorial Inc. was founded as a non-profit organisation. She was declared a National Monument and placed on the Register of National Historic Preservation. In 1979 she arrived under her own steam into San Francisco Bay and moored at Bethlehem's yard for restoration work. After eight months, she steamed around the bay on a cruise and then moored at Pier 3 East, Fort Mason Centre, astern of USS *Pampanito*. She can still steam and is open to visitors, a proud sole survivor of a wonderful class of ship. When she had been restored, she took her first annual cruise on 21st May 1980 and has been sailing on cruises ever since.

In 1994, a volunteer crew of the *O'Brien* returned the ship to the beaches of Normandy for the 50th anniversary of D-Day and the voyage was made to honour all those whose sacrifices were vital to the war effort and winning that War. This voyage, from 18th April to 23rd September 1994, included fourteen ports of call. On 6th June 1994 she was at anchor off Pointe du Hoc as a visible reminder of the fleet of over 6,000 vessels in the invasion of Normandy in 1944. The *O'Brien* was the only Normandy ship to return for the Commemoration Ceremonies.

She was dry-docked in 2006 as she has to every five years. She does regular cruises around the west coast of America and is now listed as a national historic landmark.

Her engines were used in the filming of 'Titanic'.

Contact details:

SS *Jeremiah O'Brien*, Golden Gate National Recreation Area, Fort Mason, San Francisco, California, 94123, USA.
Telephone: (415) 544.0100.
Website: www.ssjeremiahobrien.org.
She is now moored at Pier 45, Fisherman's Wharf and is open daily 9 a.m. – 4 p.m.
Closed 1st January, Thanksgiving and 25th December.

REBIRTH AND RESTORATION
1979

57

Come aboard our fully restored Liberty Ship - saved from the ship-breakers by hundreds of volunteers...

World War II service from Normandy to the far Pacific ended in 1946 when she entered the inactive Reserve Fleet in Suisun Bay, California.

Thirty three years later, Merchant Marine veterans, led by Admiral Thomas J. Patterson of the U.S. Maritime Administration, steamed the SS Jeremiah O'Brien out of the "Mothball Fleet" under her own power.

We continue to sail her as a living memorial to the men and women who built, sailed and perished on Liberty Ships during World War II. Welcome Aboard!

The National Liberty Ship Memorial is crewed entirely by Volunteers and is a Registered Historic Landmark

Plate 57 – *SS* Jeremiah O'Brien. *(Author's collection.)*

Plate 58 – *SS* Jeremiah O'Brien. *(Author's collection.)*

RUSSIAN SUBMARINES (B39) and (B427)

This ex-Russian submarine (plate 59) was sold off by the Soviet forces and purchased by the owners of *RMS Queen Mary*, at Long Beach, California, of whom she is moored alongside. She is open for visiting and is known by the Nato name of '*Foxtrot*' class of fifty-eight boats. (She is also called project 641 by the guides.)

Technical specifications:

Built in 1972, she is of 1,950 / 2,400 tonnes, 91.5 x 7.5 x 6ft in dimensions with 10 TT, six forward x four aft, or could carry forty-four mines. Fitted with three diesels of 2,000 HP and three electric motors with three props, she had 5,300 HP (submerged). Endurance was seventy days and a range of 11,000 miles. Of the fifty-eight boats built at Leningrad, seventeen were built for export, eight to India, six to Libya and three to Cuba. Several of these units were lost at sea due to defects.

The other Russian submarine (B39) is also a 'Foxtrot' class with similar fittings. She is moored at the Maritime Museum of San Diego (Plates 60 and 61).

Contact details:
Website: www.sdmaritime.org.

Plate 59 – *Russian submarine* B427 *at Long Beach, along side* Queen Mary. *(Author's collection.)*

Plate 60 – *Russian submarine* B39 *at San Diego Maritime Museum. (Author's collection.)*

Plate 61 – *Russian submarine* B39 *at San Diego Maritime Museum. (Author's collection.)*

STEAM YACHT MEDEA

This steam yacht of 130 tonnes was built in Scotland in 1904 for a wealthy owner's use, but served in the First World War as an armed yacht on harbour duties. She was then returned to her owner at the end of the First World War and continued to be used for pleasure purposes. In April 1941 she was hired by the British War Office to be a Boom Bar Vessel (BBV 4) on light harbour duties and in September 1942 she was purchased outright and used as an accommodation vessel. During the period from 1st December 1942 to March 1943 she had a Norwegian crew. She was sold from Naval Service in November 1945 and then returned to her private owners. She was finally purchased by the San Diego Maritime Museum and restored to her former Edwardian elegance and has still got her original steam engines in full working order and can sometimes be seen steaming around San Diego harbour in her full glory. She now lies at the museum site (with the Russian submarine *B39*) and is open to visitors.

Contact details:

The San Diego Maritime Museum, 1492 North Harbour Drive, San Diego, CA 92101, USA.

Website: www.sdmaritime.org.

Plate 62 – Medea *(Photo from author's collection).*

HOLLAND'S PROTOTYPE OF USS *HOLLAND* (SS-1)

This one-man submarine (Plate 63) was one of the forerunners of *SS1*, the US Navy's first submarine, the other being Holland's three-man *Finian Ram*, both of which sank in the Passiac River. She was raised in 1927 and both she and *Finian Ram* are now displayed at Paterson, NJ. This one (plate 63) is in the Patterson Museum, Broadway, Summer St, whilst *Finian Ram* is in West Side Park.

Plate 63 – *One-man submarine. (Photo courtesy of Patterson Museum).*

USS *CAIRO*

Cairo was one of the famous ironclad river gunboats built by James B. Eads, known as 'Pook Turtles' because of their ungainly appearance, and their designer, Naval constructor, Samuel Pook, who worked under the supervision of Comdr John Rodgers and Capt. Andrew Foote. These warships spearheaded the Union thrust into the South along the Mississippi River and its tributaries, which split the Confederacy and won the War in the West.

Cairo was sunk on 12th December 1862, the first victim of a 'torpedo' (mine) in combat on the Yazoo River. This was during the Yazoo Pass Expedition, a part of General Grant's wide sweep to capture strongly fortified Vicksburg – 'Gibraltar of the West'.

She was rediscovered by National Park historian, Edwin C. Bearss, and geologist, Warren Grabau, in the summer of 1956. US Navy divers and underwater demolition experts assisted with the removal of ammunition, including treacherous black powder, found in the magazine.

After restoration at Pascagoula, Miss., she will be returned to Vicksburg as the main attraction of an admirable local museum.

INTELLIGENT WHALE

This hand-cranked experimental submarine was laid down during the American Civil War and condemned in 1872. Manned by six to thirteen persons, she could submerge for several hours and make nearly five knots underwater. The plans for the submarine were originally proposed by Scovel S. Merriam, and finance and construction were by August Price and C. S. Bushnell. The main designer and operator of her was a Mr Halstead. The sinking of her and the condemnation came after his death when his heirs attempted to complete the contract without the experience that he had. She is now on display at the Navy Memorial Museum, Naval Historical Display Centre, Old Washington Naval Yard.

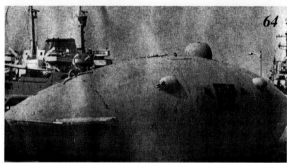

Plate 64 – Intelligent Whale *(Photo courtesy of Naval Memorial Museum, Washington Navy Yard).*
Plate 65 – *USS* Intelligent Whale.

ITALIAN TWO-MAN SUBMARINE
MAIALE (PIG)

This two-man submarine can be seen at the Naval Submarine Base in New London, USA, and another is preserved at the Submarine Museum, Portsmouth, UK. Originally built in 1936, these were what were known as manned torpedoes with electric power and joystick steering. Their greatest success was in December 1941 when they damaged the RN ships HMS *Queen Elizabeth,* HMS *Valiant* and HMS *Jervis* and the Tanker *Sagona* in Alexandria Harbour, Egypt. They worked by attaching the warhead to the bottom of the ship. Speed was about three knots at 50ft and endurance was five to six hours. The charge was 300 kg/660 lb.

A photo of this craft can be seen on Page 90. (Plate 95).

This craft at the New London (USA) Museum was originally owned by Dr Dudley Cooper and used as part of a war exhibit at the Ocean View Amusement Park, Norfolk, Virginia. In 1956 it was donated to the Mariners' Museum, Newport News VA, and then transferred to the Submarine Force Library and Museum in June 1976. The craft was restored as a historical display by the Naval Reserve Submarine Support Facility Detachment 301 at New London, USA.

There are many ship parts and artefacts preserved in the United States. Some are as follows: Submarine conning towers of USS *Parche* at Pearl Harbour; USS *Flasher* at Groton City, Conn.; USS *Balao* at Willard Park, outside the Navy Memorial Museum; USS *Flasher* at the US Naval Submarine Base at New London, Conn.; USS *Squalus* at Portsmouth Naval shipyard, Kittery, Maine; and USS *Seawolf's* torpedo alongside the Texas battleship. Another torpedo of USS *Swordfish* at St Paul, Minn.; and another from USS *Wahoo* at Wahoo, Nebraska. The masts of the ships USS *Oregon* and USS *Portland* are at Portland and USS *West Virginia* at the Campus of the University of West Virginia. Also the mainmast of the *Indiana* at Bloomington, Indiana. At Arlington Cemetery is the mainmast of the *Maine* and her foremast is at the US Naval Academy, Annapolis. The bow of USS *Michigan* is at Erie, Pa. At the submarine base at Conn. they have several guns as well as all the other exhibits there. The navigation bridge of USS *Franklin* is at Norfolk, Va. There are many more exhibits too numerous to list here as this is a book about warships, but it is nice to know that these parts are being preserved for future generations.

On the Island of Guam is preserved a two-man Japanese submarine (see Plate 50, Page 43.) which is preserved and on show at the military base there.

CONFEDERATE *SUBMARINE* *HUNLEY*

This submarine, which was sunk in the American Civil War, has been raised from the bottom and is now preserved at North Charleston, South Carolina, USA.

USS *BLUEBACK* (SS581)

At Portland, Oregon are preserved two ex USN ships, USS *Blueback* and *PT658*.

Blueback is a Barbel class submarine, built at Ingalls shipyard at Pascagoula, Mississippi, USA. Laid down 15th April 1957, launched 16th May 1959 and completed 3rd June 1960.

Technical Specifications:

Length 219ft, beam 29ft, draught 28ft, displacement 2150, surface 2,895 submerged. 6 x 21" torpedo tubes, 3x Fairbanks Morse Diesels, 3100HP electric driven, one shaft. Speed 15 surface and 25 submerged, complement 77 (eight officers, 69 men).

She was the last non-nuclear submarine to be built for the US navy and served for 31 years making her the last to be decommissioned of the non-nuclear submarines. In September 1961 she set a new record for undersea travel when she travelled underwater from Yokosuka, Japan to San Diego – a total of 5,340 nautical miles. The Oregon Museum of Science and Industry took possession of her in 1964 and she is now currently on display seven days a week.

Contact:

Oregon Museum of Science and Industry, 1945 SE Water Avenue, Portland, Oregon, 97214 3354 USA.
Phone: 503 797 4000, Fax 503 797 4500
Email: r.g.walker@omsi.edu
Website: http://omsi.edu/submarine

PT658

PT658 is a 625 series boat, launched 30th July 1945. Built by Higgins Industries boatyard at New Orleans, LA, USA. Keel laid down on 24th February 1944, launched 14th February 1945 and completed 30th July 1945.

Technical Specifications:

Length is 78.5ft, beam 20.1ft, draught 5.3ft, displacing 48 tons, crew 3 officers and 14 men. Armament 40mm Bofors, 2x twin .50 cal MG, 2 x 20mm Oerlikons, 2x MK 13 torpedos, 2 depth charges and smoke generator.

She never entered war service and was originally due to be sent to Russia but never was dispatched. She then was redesignated as a Crash Rescue Boat and finally in 1958 she was sold off to a private buyer. Since 1994 she has been in the hands of dedicated volunteers who have restored her to her former configuration.

Contact:

Save the PT Boat Inc, PO Box 13422, Portland, Oregon, 97213, USA.
To visit go to Naval & Marine Corps Reserve Centre, Swan Island, 6735 N Basin Avenue, Portland, Oregon, 97217, USA.
Telephone: 1 503 285 4566 – Fax 1 503 281 0716.
Email: wboerger@wildwoodgrp.com or theresececile@comcast.net
Website: http://www.savetheboatinc.com

USS *ALBACORE* (AGSS 569)

At Portsmouth, New Hampshire, USA lies the USS *Albacore (AG 569)*. She is one of a class and is an experimental submarine. Laid down at Portsmouth Naval Shipyard on 15th March 1952, she was launched 1st August 1953 and commissioned 5th December 1953.

Technical Specifications:

Length 204ft, beam 27.5ft, draught 18.5ft, displacement 1500 tons surface, 1850 tons submerged, no tubes. Engines 2 x GM diesels and Westinghouse electric motor. Speed 25 knots on surface, 33 submerged. Complement 5 officers and 47 men.

She was the first submarine to be built with a true submarine hull form and she was built solely for experimental work. She was laid off in 1972 and taken to the Portsmouth Submarine Memorial's dry berth where she is now open to visitors.

Contact:

Albacore Park, 600 Market Street, Portsmouth, New Hampshire, 03801, USA.
Telephone 1 603 436 3680
Email jbsergeant@aol.com
Website http://ussalbacore.org

USS *TORSK* (SS423) later (AGSS 423)

Lying at Baltimore is the submarine USS *Torsk (SS423)* later *(AGSS 423)* one of ten of the Tench class. Built at Portsmouth Navy Yard she was laid down 7th June 1944, launched 6th September 1944 and commissioned 16th December 1944.

Technical Specifications:

Of 1840 tons surface 2400 submerged, length 312ft, beam 27.2ft, draught 16.5ft 10 x 21" torpedo tubes engines four diesels 6400 shp electric motors 5400 shp two shafts speed 20 knots surface ten knots submerged, complement 85.

She made two war patrols in the Pacific and sank one freighter and two frigates, the last one being the last ship to be sunk by a US vessel in WW2 on 14th August 1945. After the war she became a training ship and was fitted with snorkel in 1950. Decommissioned on 4th March 1968 she arrived at Baltimore in 1972 as a museum ship.

Contact:

Baltimore Maritime Museum, 802 S. Caroline St, Baltimore Maryland 21231 USA
Telephone 1 410 396 3453 – Fax: 1 410 396 3393
Email admin@baltimoremaritimemuseum.org
Website www.baltimoremaritimemuseum.org

USS *MARLIN* (SST2) ex (T2)

At Omaha Nebraska lies the submarine USS *Marlin (SST2) ex (T2)* one of two of the Mackerel class built at the Portsmouth Naval Yard. She was laid down 1st April 1952, launched 17th July 1953, completed 28th November 1953.

Technical Specifications:

Displacement 303 tons surface 347 submerged, Length 131.2ft, beam 13.5ft, draught 12.2ft, one torpedo tube forward. Engines 2 x GM diesels, one shaft, one electric motor, speed eight knots, surface 9.5 knots submerged. Complement 18 (2 officers 16 men).

She and her sister boat were built solely as training boats and she was based at Key West Florida for all of her serving life. She was decommissioned in 1973 and was then taken to her present berth as a museum ship.

Contact:

Freedom Park, 2497 Freedom Park Road, Omaha, Nebraska, 68110 2745

Telephone: 1 402 444 5900 – Fax 1 402 444 6838

Email: bpaul@co.omaha.ne.us

Website: www.cityofomaha.org/parks/parks-a-facilities/specialty-parks/freedom-park

USS *DOLPHIN* (AGSS 555)

At San Diego's maritime museum is preserved the US submarine USS *Dolphin (AGSS 555)*. Built at Portsmouth Naval shipyard she was laid down 9th November 1962, launched 8th June 1968 and commissioned 17th August 1968. She is one of a class and was built for deep diving experiments.

Technical Specifications:

Displacement 800 tons standard 930tons full load, length 165ft, beam 19.3ft, draught 17ft, one torpedo tube but carried no torpedos. Engines diesel/electric (2 Detroit 12V71 diesels) 1500shp one shaft. Speed 12 knots, complement three officers, 20 men + 4-7 scientists.

She served the US navy for 44 years in an experimental capacity and was decommissioned in 1998 after undergoing a $50 million refit following a fire and it was decided to lay her off as she was no longer fit for normal use. She was donated to the museum in 1998.

Contact:

Maritime museum of San Diego, 1306 N Harbour Drive, San Diego, California 92101 USA

Telephone: 1 619 234 9153 – Fax 1 619 234 8345

Email: info@sdmatitime.org

Website: www.sdmaritime.com

USS *REQUIN* (SS 481) later (AGSS 481)

USS *Requin* (*SS 481* later *AGSS 481*) is a Tench class submarine, one of eight which is preserved at Pittsburgh built at Portsmouth Navy yard and laid down 24th August 1944, launched 1st January 1945, commissioned 28th April 1945.

Technical Specifications:

Displacement 1840 tons surfaced 2440 submerged length 308ft, beam 27ft, draught 17ft, 10 x 21" torpedo tubes six fwd four aft, engines three diesels 4800 shp, two shafts speed, 18 knots surface, 15 knots submerged, complement 84.

She was on her way to the Pacific when WW2 ended and she spent the rest of her service in training roles. She was finally laid off and presented to the Carnegie Science centre.

Contact:

USS *Requin*, Carnegie Science Centre, 1 Allegheny Ave, Pittsburgh, Pennsylvania, 15212 USA

Telephone: 1 412 237 1550 – Fax 1 412 237 3375

Email www.carnegiesciencecenter.org/default.aspx

USS *X1*

USS *X1* is to be found at Groton CT. She was an experimental vessel. Launched 7th September 1955 at Oyster Bay, Long Island, New York USA and commissioned 7th October 1955.

Technical Specifications:

Displacement 31 tons surface 36 tons submerged, length 49.2ft, beam 7ft, draught 7ft, main engines diesels 30shp + electric motors, speed 15 knots surface 12 knots submerged, complement two officers and six men. Armament none fitted.

She was the only midget submarine ever to be built for the US navy. Originally powered by a hydrogen peroxide/diesel engine but suffered an explosion in May 1957 (frequently happened in the German WW2 experimental subs) and was then converted completely to diesel/electric. She was finally decommissioned on 16th February 1973 and was then taken to the Naval Ship Research and Development Centre in Annapolis and ultimately to her present berth in April 2001.

Contact:

Submarine Force Museum, 1 Crystal Lake Rd, Groton, CT 06349 5571

Telephone: 1 800 343 0079 & 1 860 694 3558 – Fax 1 860 694 4150

Email nautilus@subasenion.navy.mil

Website: www.ussnautilus.org

Plate 66 *– Midget Submarine: 'X' Type 1962. (Photo courtesy of United States Navy.)*

USS *NAUTILUS* (SSN 571)

Also to be found here is USS *Nautilus (SSN 571)* an ex nuclear submarine. Built by the Electric Boat Co: at Groton she was laid down 14th June 1952, launched 21st January 1954 and commissioned 30th September 1954.

Technical Specifications:

Displacement 3530 tons standard 4040 submerged, length 320ft, beam 28ft, draught 22ft. Torpedo tubes 6 x 21" forward + Anti submarine torpedos. Engines two Westinghouse geared turbines 1500 shp, two shafts. Nuclear reactor one pressurised water cooled S2W (Westinghouse) Speed 20 knots on surface and submerged. Complement 10 officers and 95 men.

Nautilus was the world's first nuclear powered submarine and the nuclear capacity allowed her to remain submerged for days, weeks or months. In 1958 she sailed beneath the Artic icepack to the North Pole and broadcast her historic message to the world "Nautilus 90 North". She was decommissioned in 1980 and taken to Groton where she was built, to be preserved and is open to the public.

Contact:

As for USS *X1*.

USS *TURNER JOY* (DD951)

USS *Turner Joy (DD951)* is a Forest Sherman class destroyer built by Puget Sound Dredging Co. at Seattle Washington. Laid down 30th September 1957, launched 5th May 1958, commissioned 3rd August 1959.

Technical Specifications:

Displacement 2850 standard 4050 full load. Length 418ft, beam 45ft, draught 22ft, armament 3 x 5" 54 calibre, 2 x 3" AA. ASW weapons one ASROC eight tube launcher, 2 x triple torpedo tubes (MK 46) Engines 2 x General Electric geared turbines 70,000shp two shafts, speed 33 knots.

She served from 1960–1982 when she was laid off and in 1991 she was placed at Bremerton Historic ships display.

Contact:

Bremerton Historic Ships Association, 300 Washington Beach Ave, Bremerton, Washington 98337 5668
Telephone: 1 360 792 2457 – Fax 1 360 377 1020
Email: dd951@sinclair.net
Website: www.ussturnerjoy.org

USS *ORLECK* (DD886)

Texas has the Gearing class destroyer USS *Orleck (DD886)* preserved at Orange. She was built at Consolidated Steel Corp's yard at Orange where she now lies and was launched 12th May 1945, commissioned 15th September 1945.

Technical Specifications:

Length 390.5ft, beam 40.9ft, draught 19ft. Displacement 2425 tons standard 3480 full load, ASW Weapons one ASROC eight tube launcher, 4 x 5" 38 calibre guns, ten torpedo tubes and two drone anti submarine helicopters. Engines 2 x general Electric geared turbines 60,000shp, two shafts, boilers four Babcock & Wilcox. Speed 34 knots, complement 14 officers 260 men.

She operated in the Pacific and off of China and Japan, took part in the Atomic tests at Eniwetok and also served in Alaskan waters. Also in the Korean War and was then relegated to training and Far East duties. In 1960 she was home-ported to

Yokosuka Japan and worked in the Taiwan Strait. She was modernised in 1963 and then worked off of the coast of Vietnam. Decommissioned in 1982 she was given to Turkey and renamed TCG *Yucetepe* and served with them until 1998 when she was again decommissioned and finally was acquired for the Texas War Memorial.

Contact:

Southeast Texas War Memorial and Heritage Foundation, PO Box 3005, Orange, Texas 77631 3003
Telephone: 1 409 882 9191 – Fax 1 409 883 7795
Email: info@ussorlock.org
Website: www.ussorlock.org

USS *STEWART* (DE 238)

Also at Texas in Galverston is the Edsall class destroyer USS *Stewart (DE 238)* built by Brown Shipbuilding Co. at Houston, launched 22nd November 1942 and completed 31st May 1943.

Technical Specifications:

Length 306ft, beam 36.6ft, draught 11ft, displacement 1200 tons standard 1850 tons full load. Armament 3 x 3" 50 calibre guns, 2 x quad 40mm AA guns, ten twin 20mm AA, Hedgehog and depth charges. Engines 4 x Fairbanks Morse diesels 6000shp two shafts 21 knots. Complement 149.

She began her naval service as a 'school' ship training naval officers and escorted President Roosevelt in the presidential yacht down the Potomac River to take him to USS *Iowa* for the Casablanca conference. In 1944 she commenced North Atlantic convoys making over 30 Atlantic crossings. She was moved to the Pacific in 1945 and steamed out of Pearl Harbour on numerous exercises. Decommissioned in late 1945 and in 1974 she was donated by the US navy to Seawolf Park in Galveston.

Contact:

For visits – Seawolf Park, Pelican Island, Galveston, Texas 77552, USA
Inquiries: Cavalla Historical Foundation, RR8, Box 10, Galveston, Texas 77554, USA
Telephone: 1 409 797 5115 – Fax 1 409 744 7854
Email: macm@galvestonparkboard.org
Website: www.cavalla.org

USS *LITTLE ROCK* (CL 92) later (CLG4)

USS *Little Rock (CL 92)* later *(CLG4)*. This Cleveland class cruiser was built at Cramp's Shipbuilding Company, Philadelphia and laid down 6th March 1943, launched 27th August 1944 and commissioned 17th June 1945.

Technical Specifications:

Length 610ft, beam 66ft, draught 25ft, displacement 10670 tons standard 14600 full load, 3 x 6" guns, 2 x 5" calibre guns and later 2 x Mk2 Talaos Missile launchers. Engines 4 x general Electric geared turbines 100,000shp four shafts. Boilers 4 x Babcock and Wilcox, speed 31.6 knots, complement 1200 officers and men.

Little Rock is the only survivor of this class left and also has the distinction of also being the only 'WW' cruiser on display in the US. In 1960 she underwent a complete conversion to a guided missile cruiser at the New York Shipbuilding Corp. yard at Camden New Jersey, USA. She was struck from the navy register in 1976 and then acquired by the City of Buffalo in 1977. She is now on display at Buffalo with the other ships there – USS *Croaker* (see Page 33) and USS *The Sullivans* (see Page 70)

Contact:

Buffalo & Erie County Naval and Military Park, 1 Naval Park Cove, Buffalo, New York 14202, USA
Telephone: 1 716 847 1773 – Fax 1 716 847 6405
Email: info@buffalonavalpark.org
Website: www.buffalonavalpark.org

USS *SALEM* (CA 139)

USS *Salem (CA 139)*. This Des Moines class ship of three heavy cruisers can be found preserved at Quincy. Laid down 27th September 1946 and launched 25th March 1947 she is one of the heaviest cruisers to be built in the world.

Technical Specifications:

Displacement 17,000 tons standard 21500 full load, length 716.5ft, beam 77ft, draught 22ft. Guns 9 x 8" in three turrets, 12 x 5" in twin turrets and 18 x 3", engines geared turbines four shafts, 120,000shp, speed 28 knots, complement 1860 (war load).

For eight years she served as Flagship of the Sixth Fleet in the Mediterranean. In 1953 she was the first ship to arrive to relieve the Ionian Islands of Greece which had been hit by a bad earthquake and for this humanitarian service she was given the praise of the King and Queen of Greece. She never ever fired her guns in anger and was decommissioned in 1959 and was opened for visitors as a museum ship in May 1995 and is the meeting point for USN Cruisers Sailors Association Memorial, USS Salem Exhibit, USS Newport News Exhibit.

Contact:

United States Shipbuilding Museum, 739 Washington St, Quincy, Massachusetts 02169, USA.
Telephone: 1 617 479 7900 – Fax 1 617 479 8792
Email: seawitchskipper@aol.com
Website: www.usssalem.org

USS *KIDD* (DD 661)

USS *Kidd (DD 661)* is a WWS Fletcher class destroyer launched 28th February 1943 at the Federal Shipbuilding & Drydock Co. Kearny, New Jersey and commissioned 23rd April 1943. She is now preserved as a museum ship at Baton Rouge.

Technical Specifications:

Length 376.5ft, beam 39.5ft, draught 18ft, displacement 2050 tons standard 2750 tons full load. Armament 5 x 5" guns calibre, 5 x 21" torpedo tubes, + 40mm and 20mm AA guns and depth charges.

She was named in honour of Rear Admiral Kidd who was killed aboard his Flagship USS *Arizona* when the Japanese struck at Pearl Harbour December 7th 1941. She saw a lot of action in the Pacific and was at the Gilbert and Marshall Islands, Philippines at Leyte Gulf and Okinawa where she survived a kamikaze attack and after WWII she was deployed to Korea for that war. She was finally decommissioned in 1964 and put into the Atlantic Reserve Fleet and in 1982 she was transferred to The Louisiana Naval War Memorial Commission. She was never modernised before laying off so is in her WWII configuration.

USS Kidd Veterans' Memorial, 305 South River Rd, Baton Rouge, Louisiana 70802, USA.
Telephone: 1 225 342 1942 – Fax 1 225 342 2039
Email info@usskidd.com
Website: www.usskidd.com

USS *BARRY* (DD993)

USS *Barry (DD993)* is a Forest Sherman class of destroyer as is USS *Turner Joy* (Page 60) and her statistics are the same as that ship. She supported the 1958 Marine airborne unit that landed in Beirut, Lebanon; and in 1962 she was involved in the task force that shut off Cuba when she tried to import Russian missiles. She also served in the Vietnam conflict and in 1970 she was stationed at Athens in Greece. Decommissioned in 1982 she was made into a museum ship in 1984.

Contact:
USS *Barry*, 707 Riverside Drive S.E., Pier 2, Washington Navy Yard, DC 20374 4038
Website: www.history.navy.mil/visit/visit5.htm

USS *SLATER* (DE 766)

USS *Slater (DE 766)* of the Cannon class of Destroyer Escorts is now preserved at Albany, New York. Launched 13th February 1944 at Tampa Shipbuilding, Tampa, Florida and commissioned 1st May 1944.

Technical Specifications:
Length 306ftm, beam 39.6ft, draught 12ft, displacement 1440 tons. Armament 3 x 3" guns, 3 x twin 40mm AA, nine x 20mm AA, 24 missile hedgehog, two depth charge racks and eight K guns. 3 x 21" torpedo tubes, complement 200 men.

Slater is the only destroyer Escort on display in the US which is still afloat. She operated in the Atlantic on convoy duties and in May 1945 her torpedo tubes were removed and extra AA guns added and she was moved to the Pacific. She was decommissioned in 1946 and put into reserve but was transferred in 1951 to the Royal Hellenic Navy where she served for 42 years. Finally through the efforts of the Destroyer Escort Sailors Association, she was given to that organization by the Greek Government and then towed from Crete where she was lying to New York City's Intrepid Museum in 1993. In October of 1997 she was moved to her permanent berth at Albany New York, on the Hudson River.

Contact:

Destroyer Escort Historical Museum, USS Slater, PO Box 1926, Albany, New York 12201 1926,
Telephone: 1 518 431 1943 – Fax 1 518 432 1123
Email info@ussslater.org
Website: www.ussslater.org

USS *HAZARD* (AM 240)

USS *Hazard (AM 240)* is preserved at Omaha Nebraska and is an Admirable class Minesweeper built by Winslow Marine Railway & Shipbuilding Company, Winslow, Washington. Launched 21st May 1944 and commissioned 31st October 1944.

Technical Specifications:

Length 184.5ft, bean 33.1ft, draught 9ft. Displacement 900 tons, armament 1 x 3" gun, six x 20mm AA guns, four x 40mm AA guns, one hedgehog, four depth charge projectors and two racks.

She is the only Admirable class minesweeper left and one of the most successful of these classes. She had acoustic and wire sweepers. She escorted convoys and in March 1945 she was sent to Okinawa where she swept the waters off of Keramo Retto Point. She returned to the US at war's end and was placed in reserve and finally became a museum ship.

Contact:

See USS *Marlin* (Page 56).

PTF 3

PTF 3. This fast patrol boat was first built in Norway in 1962 as KNM *Skrei Torpedo* and then commissioned in the US navy as *PTF 3* in 1963.

Technical Specifications:

Length 80.4ft, beam 24.5ft, draught 6.10ft, displacement 69 tons, speed 43 knots, construction double diagonal Honduras planking, armament 1 x 40mm gun, 2 x 20mm guns, one .50 calibre machine gun.

She was first in the US series of NASTY class patrol boats and marked the return of wooden boats. She was sent to South East Asia for special operations and in conjunction with five other PT boats attacked installations in North Vietnam. During these raids the North Vietnamese attacked the PT boats with their own torpedo boats and then came under fire from the USS *Turner Joy* and USS *Maddox*. The following engagement became known as the Tonkin Gulf Incident. This was portrayed as an unprovoked attack on US ships and led to the escalation of the Vietnam War. Based in Danang *PTF 3* continued operation against the North Vietnam forces. She finally returned to the US in the 1970s and was then stationed at Key West, Florida. She was decommissioned in 1977 and sold off for scrap in 1978 and then was donated to the Boy Scouts in 2001. Without her engines she sat idle for nearly 25 years being moved all the time from place to place. On 25th May 2003 after a 250 mile journey being towed by tug she arrived in Edgewater, Florida. Later she was lifted out of the water and on 25th July 2003 she was taken overland to the Deland Naval Air Station Museum to be restored to her former glory.

Contact:

PRF 3 Restoration Project, Boy Scout Troop 544 Inc: PO Box 740789, Orange City, Florida 32774 7161, USA.
Telephone: 1 800 694 7161
Email info@scout544ptf.com
Website: www.ptf3restoration.org
Address to visit: Deland Naval Air Station Museum, 910 Biscayne Blvd: Deland, Florida, 32724 USA. Telephone: 1 386 738 4149.
Email: dnasmuseum@vol.com

PT 617 and *PT 796*

PT *617* and PT *796* are preserved at Battleship Cove (See Battleship *Massachusetts* Page 11). These boats were produced by ELCO and served in most theatres of the WWII but mainly in the Pacific area.

USS *LST 393*

USS *LST 393*. This landing ship is now preserved at Muskegon Milwaukee. Launched 11th November 1942 and built by Newport News Shipbuilding at Newport Mews she was commissioned 11th December 1942.

Technical Specifications:

Length 328ft, beam 50ftm, draught 10ft aft 3.5ft forward. Bow door ramp is 14ft, armament twin 40mm guns.

She took part in three invasions in WWII in the European area i.e. Sicilian, Salerno and Normandy. She was then sent back to the US to Norfolk Virginia and prepared for Pacific operations but the war ended before she took part. She was then decommissioned in New Orleans Louisiana in 1946 and sold to the Wisconsin and Michigan Steamship Company of Milwaukee. She operated as a ferryboat for vehicles on Lake Michigan with the name of *Highway 16* until 1973 when she was laid off and neglected. Finally in 2005 she was taken under the care of the USS *LST 393* Preservation Association and has now been rebuilt to her former condition. She is open for visitors seven days a week May to September.

Contact:

USS *LST 393*, 560 Mart St, Muskegon, Milwaukee 49440 1044
Telephone: 1 231 730 1477 – Fax 1 231 722 0016
Email: 82airbn@comcast.net
Website: www.1st393.org

USS *LST 325*

USS *LST 325* is another Landing Ship Tank with the same details as *LST 393* (see Page 67). She was also in the European war area and also took part in the Sicilian and Normandy landings. Decommissioned on 2nd July 1946 she was taken off of the navy register 1st September 1961. She was transferred to the Royal Hellenic Navy in 1964 and served for 36 years as HNS *Syros (L 144)*. She was given to American LST Veterans by Greece in 2000 and left Athens on 14th November 2000 and arrived at Mobile, Alabama on 10th January 2001. She is now restored to her WWII condition.

Contact:
USS LST Ship Memorial Inc., 840 LST Drive, Evansville, IN 47713
Telephone: 1 812 435 8678
Email: webskipper@1stmemorial.org
Website: www.1stmemorial.org

FENIAN RAM

Fenian Ram. This was an early experimental submarine which was launched on 1881 at Paterson, New Jersey. She was the second experimental sub. to be built by the Irishman John P Holland who built many more for several navies. It was financed by the Fenian Brotherhood, an Irish movement in the US who wanted Ireland's independence from the UK.

Technical Specifications:
Length 31ft, beam 6ft, displacement 19 tons and a crew of three men.
This submarine led to the *SS1* which was the first British submarine, now at the Museum at Gosport Hampshire UK (see Page 89).

Contact:
Paterson Museum, 2 Market St, Paterson, New Jersey 07501 1704
Telephone: 1 973 321 1260 – Fax 1 973 881 3435
Email patersonmuseum@hotmail.com
Website: www.thepatersonmuseum.com

The following vessels are thought to be preserved as stated but confirmation cannot be obtained at present and any help on these vessels would be most appreciated.

I have not listed Coastguard and similar ships or boats as they are not warships:

PBR	Mark II at Vallejo, California USA
PBR	Mark II at Bellingham, Washington, USA
LCVP	Washington, District of Columbia USA
PCF 1	Washington, District of Columbia USA
LCI (L) 713	Portland Oregon, USA
USS Monitor	Newport News, Virginia, USA
USS Potomac	Oakland, California, USA
LCI (L) 1091	Eureka, California, USA
LCM 56	Fall River, Massachusetts, USA
PT 309	Fredericksburg, Texas, USA
PACV 4	Bellingham, Washington, USA
PT 615	Kingston, New York, USA
PBR Mark II	Orlando, Florida, USA
PBR Mark II	Mobile, Alabama, USA
PBR Mark II	Hackensack, New Jersey, USA
Japanese Kaiten	Hackensack, New Jersey, USA
USS Lucid	Bradford Is., California, USA
German Seehund	Quincy, Massachusetts, USA
PTF 17	Buffalo, New York, USA
PTF 26	Rio Vista, California
USS Growler	New York, New York, USA
USS Razorback	Little Rock, Arkansas, USA
Japanese HA 19	Fredericksburg, Texas, USA

THE FOLLOWING VESSELS ARE BELIEVED TO BE PRESERVED AS STATED:

PT (TORPEDO BOAT) 309 at Fredericksburg, Texas, USA. Built by Higgins Industries Inc. Displacing thirty-four tonnes, she is 78ft long x 19ft x 5ft, has three shaft gasoline engines, 4 x 21" Torpedo tubes, 1 x 40mm and 2 x 2 mm AA guns. HP 4,050 = over forty knots with a complement of seventeen persons.

PT615 at Kingston, New York, USA. Built by Electric Boat Co., Bayonne, New Jersey (ELCO). Displacement thirty-eight tonnes, dimensions 80ft x 20.75ft x 5ft. Three shaft gasoline engines, SHP 4,050 = forty knots. 4 x 21" Torpedo tubes, 2 x 20mm AA guns. Comp: fourteen persons.

PT617 and 796 at Fall River, Massachusetts, USA. Details same as PT 615.

PT 658 at Portland, Oregon, USA. Same details as 615.

EX-LANDING CRAFT and AMPHIBIOUS:

INS Af Al Pi Chen	Haifa, Israel.
LCI(L) 713	Portland, Oregon, USA.
LCI(L) 1091	Eureka, California, USA.
LCM 56	Fall River, Massachusetts, USA.
LVGVP	Washington, District of Columbia, USA.
USS *LST 325*	Evansville, Indiana, USA.
USS *LST 393*	Muskegon, Michigan, USA.

USS *THE SULLIVANS* DD537 (ex *PUTNAM*)

This destroyer of the Fletcher class, one of 103 ships, was named after the Sullivan brothers who were all lost in the Navy in the Second World War, and is now preserved at Buffalo, New York. Built at Bethlehem's yard at San Francisco and launched on 4th April 1943, of 2,050 tonnes, she is 376.5ft overall x 39.5ft beam x 17.75ft draught. With two shaft geared turbines, SHP 60,000 = thirty-seven knots, armed with 5 x 5", 6–10 20 or 40 mm AA guns, 10 x 21" torpedo tubes and had a complement of 300 men.

USS *KIDD* (DD661)

This destroyer is of the 'Improved Fletcher' class of fifty-three ships, whose details vary little from the Fletcher class. She is preserved at Baton Rouge, Louisiana. Built by Federal General Electric, she was launched on 28th February 1943.

USS *CASSIN YOUNG* (DD793)

This destroyer, also of the same class as *Kidd*, is now preserved at Boston, Massachusetts. She was built by Bethlehem (San Pedro) Westinghouse and launched on 12th September 1943.

USS *BARRY* (DD933)

Barry is one of the 'Forrest Sherman' class of eighteen ships and is preserved at Washington, District of Columbia. Built at Bath Iron Works, she was laid down on 15th March 1954, launched on 1st October 1955 and commissioned on 31st August 1956. Of 3,950 tonnes (full load) she is 418.4ft long x 45.2ft wide x 20ft deep. With 3 x 5" single guns (as laid down), 2 x 3" AA, plus other AA weapons, 2 x triple torpedo tubes. Machinery: 3 x geared turbines (Westinghouse) 70,000 SHP = thirty-three knots. Four x Babcock & Wilcox boilers.

Also of this class is USS *Turner Joy DD951,* which is now preserved at Bremerton, Washington.

Of the Gearing class (same as *Joseph P Kennedy Jr*., see Page 28) is the *Orleck (DD886),* which is now preserved at Orange in Texas, USA.

Of the Cannon class of seventy-two destroyers' escorts is the USS S*later* (DD766), now preserved at Albany, New York, USA. Of 1,240 tonnes, 300 (wl), 306 (overall) x 36.5 x 8.75ft, three shaft diesel / electric drive, SHP 6,000 = twenty-one knots, S x 3" main guns, 6 x 40mm AA, 3 x 21" TT, complement 200. Thought to be at Long Beach, California, is the submarine USS *Recondor (SS 301)* of the 'Gato' class.

USS *LEXINGTON* (CV16)

At Corpus Christi, Texas, USA, is the aircraft carrier USS *Lexington* (ex-*Cabot*). Of the same class of ships as USS *Hornet, Intrepid* and *Yorktown*, she was laid down at Bethlehem Steel Co., Quincy on 15th July 1941 and was completed on 17th March 1943.

Also thought to be preserved is the heavy Cruiser USS *Salem* at Quincy, Massachusetts (CA 139). Of the Des Moines class, she was laid down at Bethlehem, Quincy on 25th March 1947 so saw no Second World War service.

Of 17,000 tonnes (21,500 full load) her dimensions are length 716.5ft (overall) x 75.5ft x 26ft (max), guns 9 x 8" 55 cal in triple turrets, 1 2 x 5 " 38 cal in twin mounts,

20 x 3" 50 cal and 12 x 20 mm AA armour 8"–6" on side + 2" on decks. Machinery, geared turbines, four shafts. SHP: 120,000 = thirty-three knots. Boilers Babcock & Wilcox, Fuel 2,600 tonnes. Complement 1,860 (war).

Another cruiser thought to be preserved at Buffalo, New York, is USS *Little Rock* (CL 92) of the Cleveland class of ships. She was laid down at Cramp's yard on 27th August 1944 and eventually was reclassified as LCG4. Of 10,000 tonnes (13,000 full load) she is 610ft long (overall) x 66ft x 25ft (max). Guns 12 x 6" 47 cal in triple turrets, 12 x 5" 38 cal paired, up to 28 40 mm AA and 19 x 20 mm AA with three aircraft, armour 5'–1.5" side, 2" deck. Machinery, geared turbines, four shafts, SHP 100,000 = thirty-three knots. Boilers: eight Babcock & Wilcox, 2,000 tonnes of oil fuel, complement 900 (peace), 1,200 (war).

The carers of the above ships were contacted by the author for more details (service history, viewing times etc.) but no reply was received from them.

USS *HARVEST MOON*

The Flagship of Rear Admiral John A. Dahlgren, ordnance expert and the Commander of the South Atlantic Blockading Squadron, *Harvest Moon* was sunk in Winyah Bay near Georgetown, South Carolina, on 1st March 1865, by a Confederate 'Torpedo' (mine). The state of South Carolina and Patriotic groups there plan to raise her, display and preserve her as a Civil War Monument.

67

Plate 67 – USS Harvest Moon. *Photo courtesy of Naval History Division Navy, Department, Washington DC.*

HMS *BELFAST*

HMS *Belfast* is a 6" gun cruiser and is of the Improved Southampton class. Her keel was laid on 10th December 1936 and, as Job 1,000 in Harland and Wolff's Shipyard, she was finished on 3rd August 1939 and commissioned on 5th August 1939.

Belfast is one of two ships built in this class. She is of the improved Southampton class and was practically rebuilt after she sustained heavy damage from a German magnetic mine, and this increased her displacement to 11,550 tonnes from the original 10,000 tonnes, as she was built. Her sister ship, *Edinburgh*, was lost on the Arctic convoys when carrying gold from Russia, but some of the gold was salvaged many years later, although some still remains in her aft magazines as it was considered too dangerous to attempt to remove it by shifting the ammunition, which was in a dangerous state. She served in the Korean theatre of war and returned to Portsmouth, her home port. Put into reserve, she was finally put up for sale and a fund was raised to buy her for preservation. The Belfast Trust was formed and the money raised to buy her, and she was dry-docked for cleaning and modifications, and then towed to Tower Bridge where she now lies. Eventually ownership was transferred to the Imperial War Museum, who do not allow anyone to stay overnight on her.

Technical specifications:

Her displacement is 11,550 tonnes, length 613ft, 6"overall x 66ft, 5" x draught 17.3", guns 12 x 6", 8 x 4" + 20 and 40mm AA, Armour of 3" on side 4" CT Turrets 2.5". Six Torpedo tubes in triples. Parsons-geared Turbines x 4 shaft. SHP 80,000 = thirty-two knots, eight x Admiralty three Drum boilers. With a complement of 847 (peacetime), on 9th October 1939 she captured the German liner SS *Cape Norte,* which was disguised as the Swedish liner SS *Anaconda* and was attempting to get back to Germany. On 21st November 1939 she was very badly damaged by a magnetic mine in the Firth of Forth and was in dockyard hands for twenty-eight months, during which time she had many modifications done to her. She was involved in the sinking of the Battle cruiser *Scharnhorst* on 26th December 1943 and she also took part on D-Day. At the end of War in Europe she went to Sydney and helped in the evacuation of Allied POWs from the Japanese and then remained in the Far East until 15th October 1947 when she was paid off to the Reserve Fleet in Portsmouth. She was re-commissioned on 22nd September 1948 and went to Belfast to receive the silver bell that is now proudly displayed on her quarterdeck. On 23rd October 1948 she sailed for the Far East and arrived in Hong Kong at the end of December. She took part in the bombardment of North Korean targets. In October 1950 she was ordered back to the UK and re-commissioned to return back to the Korean conflict. In 1952 she returned to the UK and was put into Reserve for three years, modernised, and re-commissioned on 12th May 1959, and from then until 1962 was in the Far East again. In 1961 she provided the guard for the lowering of the Union flag in Tanganyika. By then she had steamed nearly half a million miles. She was saved from the scrapyard by Rear Admiral Sir Morgan Giles, who formed a committee to buy her. The money was raised; she was bought and arrived in London. The author had the pleasure of working on her, when, with other ex-Navy men of the Nautical Club in Birmingham, we helped at weekends and we stayed on board her in the Chief's mess with the Warders. However, when the Imperial War Museum eventually took her over, they forbade the overnight stays so we stopped going to her and no one is allowed to stay overnight on her. She is now moored on the River Thames in London and well preserved. She is open for visitors and is No. 123 on the National Register of Historic Vessels.

Contact:
Website: http:/hmsbelfast.iwm.org.uk/

68

Plate 68 – HMS Belfast *(Author's collection).*
Plate 69 – HMS Belfast *(Author's collection).*
Plate 70 – HMS Belfast *(Author's collection).*

HMS *VICTORY*

HMS *Victory* is the oldest complete preserved warship in the world and is still a fully commissioned warship of the Royal Navy, being the flagship of the CinC (Portsmouth) and all Court Martials are still held aboard her. She was built at Chatham on 7th May 1765 as a First Rate of the line of one hundred guns. Her best known action was at Trafalgar on 21st October 1805, when Admiral Horatio Nelson defeated all the Spanish and French fleet using the *Victory* as his flagship, on which he died. She was finally laid up in Portsmouth Harbour in 1822 and remained there serving in many capacities, but then it was decided, because she had such a good history, she would be preserved. However, her below waterline hull was in a bad state, so it was decided to put her into a dry dock. After lying in the harbour for one hundred years, she was towed to her resting place in the dockyard (where she now is) on 12th January 1922. After six years of work on her (1922-1928) and the sum of £100,000 being spent on her after public subscription, the ship was restored to the appearance that she had at Trafalgar in 1805, and she is in a beautiful condition in her dry dock and, although open for visitors all year long in the dockyard, she is still a fully commissioned warship on the Navy's books and still flies the White Ensign. The Figurehead is a carved crowned shield of the Royal Arms, which is supported by two cupids. Not all of her cannons are the originals – some of them are made of wood – but there are several that can be and are fired on 'Navy Days'. Her keel is 150ft long and 20" square, and is made of teak. The hull is of English oak and has outer and inner 'skins' and is two feet thick and below the waterline she was protected by copper sheathing, added after the ship was launched in 1765. She now rests on steel cradles made to fit her sides. During the Second World War a Nazi bomb exploded between the ship's side and the dock wall, blowing a large hole in the underpart of the hull near to the port bow, a miraculous escape for such a lovely proud ship. This damage can still be seen by the splintered stonework of the dockside. The overall length of the ship is, from figurehead to the Taffrail, 226ft, 6" and the extreme beam is 52ft, 6". The heaviest guns (thirty-two pounders) are on the lower gun deck, twenty-four pounders on the middle deck and twelve pounders on the upper deck. She is still in her black and yellow colours of Trafalgar. This ship is in pristine condition in her dockyard home and is open to visitors. She is well worth a visit and if you should visit her, also visit the *Mary Rose*, the *Warrior* and also the ex-Navy *M33* in the dry dock near her to make a really good day of ship sightseeing in Portsmouth. See Pages 79, 77 and 82.

1765	Completed but then put straight into reserve.
1778	Commissioned as a flagship of Admiral Keppel after the outbreak of the American War of Independence.
1780	Her bottom was plated with 3,923 copper sheets, which weighed 17 tons.
1781	Admiral Kempenfelt's flagship at his victory at Ushant.
1782	Flagship of Admiral Howe at the relief of Gibraltar by Marines.
1793	Flagship of Lord Hood, C in C Mediterranean.
1797	Flagship of Admiral Jervis at the victory at Cape St Vincent.
1803	After an overhaul refit for three years, sails for the Mediterranean as Nelson's Flagship.
1805	Battle of Trafalgar and death of Nelson.
1808	
–1812	Flagship in the Baltic campaigns.
1824	Flagship of the Port Admiral at Portsmouth.
1831	Put for scrapping but saved by 1st Sea Lord Admiral Thomas Hardy.
1889	Flagship of C in C Portsmouth.
1922	Dry-docked for preservation.
1928	Open to the public.
1941	Damaged by a bomb between dock and hull, but repaired.

Plate 71 – *HMS* Victory *(Author's collection).*

Plate 72 – *HMS* Victory *(Author's collection).*

Plate 73 – *Stern cabin on HMS* Victory. *(Author's collection.)*

HMS *WARRIOR*

HMS *Warrior* was an iron armed ship of 9,210 tonnes, 380 x 58.5ft, with 11 x 110 pounders, 26 x 68 pounders, built at T.I.W. Blackwall, on 29th December 1860 and she was of a new design using iron and thus at a stroke outdating and making obsolete all the Navy's sailing warships. She became a depot ship in July 1902 and was renamed

Vernon III in March 1904. She was then hulked as *Warrior* in 1923 and then renamed *C77* when she became an oiling jetty in 1945. She was finally put up for disposal and her future looked very bleak, in fact she was pretty certain to be scrapped, but then a group of very dedicated people stepped in and it was decided to buy her and then rebuild her to her former glory. She was towed to Hartlepool and then stripped and gutted and sat alongside the jetty for some time whilst the money was raised to rebuild her. Finally the rebuild started and she was over a period rebuilt to her previous beautiful lines of a steam / sailing ship. When she was completely rebuilt, she was then towed to Portsmouth where she was moored outside the dockyard and opened to visitors. She is now well visited and people pore over her as she is so impressive in her berth. Well worth a visit and a very interesting exhibit, she is moored just outside the dockyard gates, giving off an air of days gone by. Her owners should be congratulated for their efforts to save and rebuild her and she is a credit to them, a very fine, wonderfully preserved, ship.

Plate 74 – HMS Warrior *at Portsmouth. (Author's collection.)*
Plate 75 – HMS Warrior *as a hulk at Hartlepool prior to reconstruction. (Author's collection.)*

Plate 76 – HMS Warrior *at Portsmouth. (Author's collection.)*

Plate 77 – HMS Warrior *at Portsmouth. (Author's collection.)*

Plate 78 – HMS Warrior *at Portsmouth. (Author's collection.)*

Plate 79 – Mary Rose *being lifted from seabed at Spithead. (Author's collection.)*

THE *MARY ROSE*

The *Mary Rose* is a wooden warship from the fleet of Henry VIII. She was laid down and launched in 1510/1511 and was named after the King's younger sister. She was flagship of the Lord Admiral and said to be a great favourite with Henry. She played a very important part in the War of 1512–1514 with the French and when war broke out again in 1545, she was set to play a leading part. It was in that conflict when disaster struck. It was when the French fleet attempted to attack Portsmouth, she then sailed with the fleet against them, but whilst changing her course to attack the French, she heeled over with her gun ports still open; the water poured into her and she rolled right over and sank. It is said that Henry was watching this from Southsea Castle at this time and, watching his fleet's movements, he saw her sink and was heartbroken. She then lay in the Solent, sinking deeper and deeper into the mud, until an independent diver who had read about her demise, spent many years trying to find her and finally succeeded in discovering where she lay. It was decided to attempt to lift her to the surface and the money was raised for this. The final lift of the half of the hull that was still left was witnessed by Prince Charles, who had taken a keen interest in this vessel. It was in 1982 that she was finally raised by the use of Transportation Barge, *Tow 1*, and she was then taken into Portsmouth and transferred to a cradle of steel that had been specially fabricated for her. She now rests in the Ship Hall, near to HMS *Victory*, and is currently being rebuilt to her original design and specifications. Many were the artefacts and valuable pieces that were found in her hull and then restored. She can now be viewed if visiting HMS *Victory* or other places in Portsmouth dockyard and is well worth the visit. It is hoped to eventually fully restore her with the other timbers that have been salvaged from her old resting place in the Solent.

Plate 80 – Deck of HMS Warrior *(Author's collection.)*

HMS *CAROLINE*

Caroline is one of a class of six ships built between 1914 and 1915. She was laid down on 14th January 1914 at the Belfast yard of Cammell-Laird's and completed in December.

Technical specifications:

Of 3,750 tonnes, dimensions are 445.7ft overall x 41.5ft x 14ft draught. 3 x 6", 2 x 3" AA, 1 MG, 4 x 21" TT in pairs. Parsons Turbines with eight Yarrow boilers. Her war complement was 325 men. She took part in several night actions after the Battle of Jutland but on 1st April 1924 she was reduced to Reserve Status and became an RNVR drillship in Belfast, Northern Ireland, where she is to this day. She is not open for tourism but is still a Royal Navy registered ship on their Reserve Fleet. She is ship numbered certificate 430 on the Register of National Historic Ships.

Plate 81 *– HMS* Caroline *(Photo courtesy of National Historic Ships).*

HM MONITOR (M33)

The *Monitor M33* was laid down under the First World War emergency estimates at Harland and Wolff's shipyard, Belfast, on 22nd May 1915.

Technical specifications:

Of 535 tonnes with HP 400 = ten knots, her machinery is by Workman Clark with triple expansion engines and two screws. She had Yarrow boilers and carried forty-five tonnes of fuel oil. She had 2 x 6" and 1 x 6 pounder guns. She served during the First World War in the Dardenelles, the Aegean and White Seas. In 1919 she was converted to a minelayer and carried fifty-two mines and on 1st December 1925 she was re-named as *Minerva* when she became a tender to HMS *Vernon* at Portsmouth. She was hulked just before the outbreak of the Second World War and was in use then as a workshop and she was then re-named *C23*. She survived the War and in 1995 was taken to Hartlepool where she was then to be rebuilt in her original war configuration as the *Monitor M33*. She was finally completed and then towed back to Portsmouth and now lies in a dry dock nearby HMS *Victory*, a proud survivor of her age. She is now restored and a credit to the dedicated people who have done her restoration and it is hoped she will now pursue a peaceful and fulfilling life as a museum ship in Portsmouth's increasing historical fleet of well preserved ships.

82

Plate 82 – M33 *at Hartlepool under restoration. (Author's collection.)*
Plate 83 – M33 *in her dry dock at Portsmouth. (Author's collection.)*
Plate 84 – Monitor *in Portsmouth dockyard as she has been repainted in her WWII dazzle colours. Photo courtesy of Ian A White.*
Plate 85 – Monitor *in Portsmouth dockyard as she has been repainted in her WWII dazzle colours. Photo courtesy of Ian A White.*
Plate 86 – Monitor *in Portsmouth dockyard as she has been repainted in her WWII dazzle colours. Photo courtesy of Ian A White.*

Note the bow of *HMS Foudroyant* (*HMS Trincomalee*) behind *M33,* also being re-built at Hartlepool. See Page 92.

HMS *ONYX* (S21)

Onyx is one of the Oberon class submarines to be preserved (also preserved are *Ocelot*, see Page 95, HMAS *Ovens*, see Page 116. and HMAS *Onslow*, see Page 114.). *Onyx* was laid down at the Cammel Laird's yard, Birkenhead on 16th November 1964, launched on 16th August 1966 and completed on 20th November 1967.

Technical specifications:

Of 1,610 tonnes (submerged 2,030), her dimensions are 241 x 26.5 x 18ft, 8 x 21" TT (six bow, two stern) with two ASR 1, sixteen VMS Diesels, and two electric motors x two shafts, and a complement of sixty-eight. She saw much service and this class of subs were well liked by the men who served in them (so I am led to believe) and they were 'follow-ons' of the earlier Porpoise class, which pre-dated them. At the end of her service with the Navy she was then put up for disposal and for 'sale by public auction' and she was then bought by 'The Warship Preservation Trust' in Liverpool in 1991, towed to Liverpool and then put on display for visiting by the public. Unfortunately, that organisation has now gone into liquidation and *Onyx* has been bought by a Mr Mullins, of Barrow, for a reported £100,000. She will be on display at her building place in Barrow as part of a new hotel complex that he is in the process of developing at Barrow and he has described her to reporters "As icing on the cake for that development". She was towed in June 2007 from Liverpool's Victoria Docks to arrive in time for the 'Barrow Festival at Sea' on 17th to 18th June.

Plate 87 – HMS Onyx *(Crown copyright).*

HMS *PLYMOUTH* (F126)

Plymouth is a frigate of the Rothesay class. Built at Devonport dockyard, she was laid down on 1st July 1958, launched on 20th July 1959 and completed on 11th May 1961.

Technical specifications:

She is of 2,800 tonnes full load, 370 overall x 41 x 17.3ft. She carried one 'Wasp' helicopter, 1 x 4 Seacat and 2 x 6 x 3" mark 3 rockets. 2 x 4.5" guns, 2 x 20mm AA. 1 x 'Limbo' three-barrelled DC mortar. Her engines are of two double reduction geared turbines x two shafts, 30,000 SHP = thirty knots, two Babcock & Wilcox boilers, oil fuel of approximately 400 tonnes. Complement 235.

Similar to the 'Whitby' class, but with modifications. She was reconstructed at Rosyth dockyard under the then programme where all ships of this class were to be modernised in 1966-72 and she was then put up 'for disposal' by the end of 1985. When put up for sale, she was finally bought by The Warship Preservation Trust and taken to Liverpool but since they went into liquidation she has a most uncertain future. The latest news of her fate appears to be that the City Council of Plymouth are attempting to raise the money to buy her and move her down to that city of her name. It is to be hoped that they will be successful in this and that she will be saved from the fate of the wrecker's yard. It appears that all her equipment on board (apart from her steam plant) is in working order. Her main generators are also in full working order but their fuel needs of them make them uneconomical to use. She just needs a 'wash and brush up' to make her ready for visitors.

Plate 88 – HMS Plymouth *(Picture CPO Pete Holdgate).*

LCT 7074 *(LANDFALL)*

This Second World War LCT (Landing Craft Tank, but referred to in the Navy as Tank Landing Craft) was built by Hawthorn Leslie at Hepburn and launched on 6th April 1944. She is of all welded construction.

Technical specifications:

Length 187.3ft, Beam 38.8ft, displacement 500 tonnes, depth of 4ft. She was used in the D-Day invasion and at War's end was sold out. She was then named 'Landfall' and was berthed at Salthouse Dock near Pier Head, Liverpool, where she became the club for the Master Mariners in 1947. Since they discontinued use of her, she has fallen into bad disrepair and is now abandoned at Birkenhead. She is the last surviving Second World War LCT in existence, but the future looks very bleak for her.

Plate 89 – LCT 7074 (Photo courtesy of National Historic Ships).

HMS *STALKER* ex (LST 3515)

This vessel, which was laid down by Yarrow's at their yard at Esquimalt and launched on 16th December 1944 and renamed *Stalker* in 1947, is lying at Pounds ship-breaking yard in Southampton, England, and is in a dilapidated condition but a group of dedicated people, called 'The Maritime Steam Restoration Trust', headed by an ex-engineroom man of the Royal Navy named Malcolm Tattersall, are attempting to raise the money needed to purchase her and restore her to her original condition. They hope that if they can get her and restore her, they will run cruises to European ports. Funds are being raised to buy two new screws, getting the boilers certified and sorting out the two Canadian Pacific engines.

Stalker is one of a large class of LSTs but at War's end only twenty-three were retained by the Navy and their numbers deleted whilst they were given names. Three were *Stalker* (Ex LST 3515), *Tracker* (Ex LST 3522) and *Lofoten* (Ex LST 3027). Most of the others of this class were given to other Navies or converted and became 'Empire' ships and many were sold to private companies.

Technical specifications:

They were of 2,140 tonnes, 5,000 full load, 347.5ft overall x 55.2 x 4.7.8 x 20mm Oerlikon AA guns, triple expansion, two shafts, 5,500 HP = thirteen knots, two Admiralty three drum boilers, oil fuel 1,400 and a complement of 115 officers and men. *Stalker* was designated as a submarine support ship in 1958. *Lofoten* became a harbour accommodation ship in 1958 and was then converted into the Royal Navy's first helicopter support ship in 1964. *Tracker* was also a harbour accommodation ship but was then converted into a net and boom carrier in 1964. They were all disposed of by 1968. It is to be hoped that 'The Maritime Steam Restoration Trust' will be successful and be able to restore her to take her place amongst all the other preserved warships.

HMS *BRONNINGTON* (M1115)

This minehunter of the Ton class is also at Liverpool and her future is in grave doubt. Her Captain at one time was Prince Charles. She was laid down on 30th May 1951, launched on 19th March 1953, and completed on 4th June 1954 by Cook, Welton and Gemmell. See 108.

HMS *UNICORN*

HMS *Unicorn* is one of the Leda class of frigates based on the French frigate, *Hebe*, which was captured in 1782. She was classed as a fifth rate forty-six. Her keel was laid down in February 1822 on No. 4 slip at Chatham Dockyard and she was launched on 30th March 1824.

Technical specifications:

Of 1,084bm, 151.5 x 40.5 x 13.11ft. She saw no action and was immediately roofed over and laid up in reserve.

In 1857 she was lent to the War Office and used as a powder hulk at Woolwich until 1862 when she was laid up again, this time at Sheerness. She was then selected to be a drillship for the RNR and in November of 1873 she was towed to Dundee where she replaced HMS *Brilliant*. In 1906, *Unicorn* was taken over by the new RNVR and when the Second World War ended she reverted back to the RNR. In 1939, a new carrier was named *Unicorn* so she was renamed *Unicorn II*. In 1941 she was again renamed, this time to HMS *Cressy,* but in 1959, when the carrier *Unicorn* was scrapped, she reverted to her original name again. She was berthed at Earl Gray Dock, but when this dock was to be filled in for the Tay Road Bridge, it was decided to scrap her. Happily, Captain Anderson, a former captain of *Unicorn,* came to her rescue and saved her (God bless him!) and she was moved to a new berth down river. 1967 saw Tay division's new HQ being built and again her future looked bleak, but a Captain Stewart started a campaign to get her permanent preservation and then in September 1968, The Unicorn Preservation Society was formed, chaired by Lord Dalhousie. On 26th September 1968, HRH Prince Philip accepted *Unicorn* from the Navy on behalf of the new society. She is now at the Victoria Dock, Dundee and it is hoped that money will be made available from the Heritage Lottery Fund to restore her to the condition of a frigate of the Royal Navy of her time.

90

91

Plate 90 – *HMS* Unicorn *(Author's collection)*.

Plate 91 – *HMS* Unicorn *(Author's collection)*.

Plate 92 – *HMS* Unicorn *(Author's collection)*.

GERMAN ONE-MAN SUBMARINE

This one-man German submarine is at the Imperial War Museum in London. It is 6.25 tonnes, has two external torpedoes of 21" diameter and its speed was six-and-a-half knots. They were used unsuccessfully against the D-Day ships at Normandy and came too late in the War to be of any practical use.

Plate 93 – *German One Man Submarine (Author's collection)*.

HM SUBMARINE *ALLIANCE*

The *Alliance* is of the 'A' class; she was laid down on 13th March 1945, at Vickers Armstrong, Barrow, launched on 28th July 1945 and completed on 14th May 1947.

One of a class of forty-six boats, of which only sixteen entered service in the Royal Navy, all launched too late for the Second World War. Her sister ship *Affray* along with *Ambush* set a then world record for underwater submergence in 1947. *Affray* was lost at Hurd Deep (Channel Islands) when her snorkel was ripped off by a merchant ship. There were no survivors.

Technical specifications:

Of 1,620 tonnes (submerged), 28.66 x 22.25 x 17ft, 1 x 4" gun, 10 x 21" TT (six bow and four stern), eight cylinder diesel and electronic motors, HP 4,300 = eighteen knots. Complement of sixty to sixty-eight. Designed for service in the Pacific, of all welded construction.

Like the rest of her class, she saw sterling service until later models of submarines came into use and the class became obsolete to the Royal Navy. She was deleted in 1973 and after many people (including the author) worked hard to raise the money, she was then purchased and presented to the Submarine Museum at Gosport, Hampshire, where she now lies on dry land and open to visitors. The author's uncle served on her and helped to prepare her for exhibition and his name can be seen in the engine room, i.e. Tommy Tucker.

Plate 94 *– HM Submarine* Alliance *(Author's collection).*

HM *SUBMARINE* (X24)

Displacing twenty-seven tonnes, this class of midget submarine were the ones that disabled the *Tirpitz* in Alten Fijord in Norway. She is 51 x 5.5ft, with two explosive side charges, and carried a crew of four men. This one was used as a training submarine for the rest of the class and she was then discarded in October 1945 but she was luckily saved. She is now at the Submarine Museum in Gosport and has been split open to see the insides and it makes one realise how brave these men were to be in such a cramped space. They were towed by a 'Mother' submarine and then cast off to make their own way to the target.

She has the distinction of being the only surviving submarine to have been at the D-Day beaches, with her sister boat *X20*.

Plate 95 – *Midget submarine X24 (Author's collection).*

ITALIAN *'MAIALE' (PIG)* TWO-MAN CHARIOT

For details of this two-man Italian Chariot turn to Page 42 for full details.

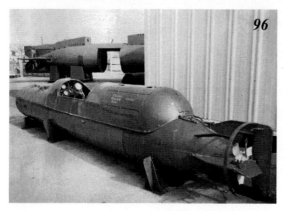

Plate 96 – *Italian two-man Chariot (Author's collection).*

HM SUBMARINE *HOLLAND* (No. 1)

This submarine, which is now preserved at the Submarine Museum at Gosport, Hants, is number one of five of the Holland class, which were the first submarines in the Royal Navy. They were of the design by Holland who built the first ones for the US Navy and this one was built the same.

Technical specifications:

Built in 1902, she was of 120 tonnes submerged displacement, with petrol four cylinder motors for the surface and accumulators for submerging. HP was 190 and her top speed was eight knots. She is 63 x 11.5 x 11.5ft, has one bow tube and an endurance of only three hours. She had long periscopes but a conning tower not worth mentioning. Her speed was controlled by advancing or retarding the spark on the engine and by cutting out cylinders to use the compression as braking power. The later '*Hollands*' (H21-52) were built in 1917, but this one is the first. She was eventually retired and languished for a while in Portsmouth Dockyard when it was decided to scrap her and whilst she was being towed to the scrapyard, she foundered in the English Channel. She lay there for many years and then a group of dedicated men decided to raise her from the seabed. This was done and she was then placed in the Submarine Museum where she now lies and is open to visitors.

97

Plate 97 – The bow torpedo tube. (Author's collection.)
Plate 98 – The stern screw. (Author's collection.)
Plate 99 – Starboard side entry. (Author's collection.)

HMS *TRINCOMALEE* ex (FOUDROYANT)

Trincomalee was laid down as a frigate in 1816 at Wadia Shipyard, Bombay, India. She was built there with her sister ship, HMS A*mphirite*, of Malabar Teak (which ultimately saved her). She was one of forty-seven Leda class frigates of thirty-eight guns. Her building was delayed by the plans being lost on HMS *Java,* which was sunk by USS *Constitution.* A second set of plans arrived two years later and so she was built. She then reached Britain in 1819 but was put straight into reserve (Ordinary as it was then called) and stayed that way for twenty-six years in Portsmouth Harbour. In 1845 her stern was modified and she became a twenty-six gun Corvette. In 1847 she was in the West Indies and then in the Crimean War and then went to the Pacific when she was again paid off in 1857. Three years later she was re-commissioned as a drill ship for Royal Naval Volunteers. Between 1860 and 1897, she was moored without her masts and with some deckhouses on her upper deck, at the *City of Sunderland,* then moved to Hartlepool and then finally to Southampton. She was bought to take the place of the training ship, *Foudroyant* (which two years earlier had foundered) by a Mr Wheatly Cobb. He then had her moored at Falmouth and later at Milford Haven and she then wound up once more at her old city of Portsmouth. On Cobb's death in 1932, she was then taken over by the Implacable Committee of the Society for Nautical Research and then moored alongside the old hulk of HMS *Implacable*, (the ex-French ship *Duguay-Trouin*) which was on loan to Cobb and which was later taken out and scuttled on 2nd December 1949 off the Owers. It took several days to clean her timbers from the sea where they were floating. During the Second World War she became a training ship for the Sea Cadets and the author had the pleasure of going aboard her for a week's training; rough but enjoyable! In 1947, she became an adventure training ship for Sea Cadets, and other sorts of youth groups who wished to use her. She was moored (see Plates 100 and 103) from 1957 to 1987 at the entrance to Haslar Creek, but due to the danger of being rammed by a submarine, she was moved to a more northerly laid mooring. Training was finally stopped on her due to her bad condition and in 1987 she was transferred by the Foudroyant Trust to Hartlepool (see Plate 101) to a yard there and she went to Jackson's Wharf to be rebuilt.

She was transported to Hartlepool (see Plate 101) by a special chartered barge which used most of the Fund's cash, leaving it in a perilous position. There ensued a period of fundraising to pay for the ship to be rebuilt. She remained at Hartlepool, a port she had occupied in 1862 and 1877. The estimated cost of restoration was £5 million, 1.5 million of which was donated by Teesside Development Corporation and Hartlepool Borough Council. It was decided to restore her to her original 1817 condition but to retain some of her 1847 features. In 1989 she was moved alongside PSS *Wingfield Castle*, which has been restored to her original condition as a paddle steamer and restoration commenced in 1990. During 1990 to 1992, the team's task was to remove certain features that had been installed when she was a training ship, and forty-eight of these were removed, the superstructure above the quarter deck was completely removed and about fifty skips of rubbish were taken from her. Eighty tonnes of ballast were also removed, cleaned and stored. A large steel frame was erected over the hull so that restoration could proceed in all weathers, 140 frames were replaced, leaving only four originals. Opepe wood was used due to its similarity to the Malabar Teak. In 1992 the Foudroyant Trust became The Trincomalee Trust and in July the name change was officially approved and The Duke of Edinburgh became the Trust's Patron. Between 1993 and 2001 the ship was dry-docked, re-coppered and replica steel masts took the place of the original wooden ones and lifts were installed between decks for disabled visitors. Replica cannons were also installed as well as an audio system for the benefit of visitors.

Despite her extensive restoration, she is still 65% original due to her original Malabar Teak still being of high quality.

She is now the focal piece in the Hartlepool Maritime Experience. She is presently moored at Jackson's Dock, Maritime Avenue, Hartlepool.

Contact:
Email: office@hms-trincomalee.co.uk

100

101

Plate 100 – *Author's collection.*

Plate 101 – *Author's collection.*

Plate 102 – *Photo courtesy of the HMS Trincomalee Trust.*

Plate 103 – Trincomalee *(ex-Foudroyant) at Portsmouth prior to her re-building. She was a cadet training ship at Portsmouth. (Author's collection.)*

HMS *CAVALIER*

One of a class of twenty-six wartime destroyers, *Cavalier* is seen here berthed at Southampton but she was then moved to Brighton, then Hebburn in Tyneside, and finally to Chatham where she is now preserved by the Chatham Historic Dockyard Trust, along with SM *Ocelot* and HMS *Gannet* (see Page 100 Plate 108).

Cavalier is the only remaining destroyer of the British fleet of Second World War vintage and is one of a class of twenty-six ships that were of the Ca, Ch, Co and Cr classes. They were of an emergency war design with a hull design modified on the 'J' class destroyers. They were built as four flotillas, i.e. Crescent, Chequers, Cossack and Caesar classes. There is very little difference in the Caesar and Zambesi classes. Two (*Crescent* and *Crusader*) were transferred to the Royal Canadian Navy, and four were sold to Norway. Two were built at Clydebank, two at Denny's shipyard, four at Scott's, three at Stephen's, four at Thornycroft, two at Vickers Armstrong (Tyne), five at White's and four at Yarrow. They were a good class of ship that did sterling work but at War's end were put into reserve and finally scrapped, but luckily the dedicated people who preserved *Cavalier*, bought her, and thanks to them she is now proudly displayed as a tribute to all the men who sailed in them and the people who saved her from the wreckers.

She is now a memorial to the 143 British Destroyers and over 11,000 lost at sea during the Second World War.

Technical specifications:

Of 2,250 tonnes at full load, she is 362.75 x 35.66 x 16ft, 4 x 4.5" guns, 4 x 40mm and 4 x 20mm AA, 4 x 21" TT. Parsons two shaft geared turbines, two x Admiralty three drum boilers. Complement 186. Was laid down on 28th February 1943, launched on 7th April 1944 and completed on 22nd November 1944. She had escorted Arctic Convoy RA64, and also escorted troopships across the Atlantic and then went to the Pacific at the end of the Second World War. When she raced HMS *Rapid* and won, she became the fastest ship in the Fleet. She was de-commissioned in 1972 and it was decided to try to save her as a memorial to the 153 destroyers and their men lost in the Second World War.

Also preserved at Chatham is the 'O' class submarine *Ocelot*.

Plate 104 – Destroyer Cavalier *at Southampton (Author's collection).*

HMS *OCELOT* (S17)

This submarine of the 'Oberon' class is one of thirteen built for the Royal Navy and the second of the class to be laid down; a fourteenth one was laid down as *Onyx* but was completed and launched as *Ojibwa* for the Royal Canadian Navy.

Technical specifications:

Displacement of 1,610 tonnes, standard 2,030 surface, 2,410 submerged. Length 241pp, 295.2 overall, beam 26.5, 18ft, 8 x 2 " draught, 8 x 21" homing torpedoes, Engines two ASR 1, sixteen VMS diesels; 3,680 BHP; two electric motors, 6,000 SHP, two shafts electric drive. Speed was twelve knots (surface), seventeen submerged, crew sixty-eight (six officers and sixty-two men) *Ocelot* was laid down on 17th November 1960, launched on 5th May 1962, and completed on 31st January 1964. For the first time in British submarines, she had plastic used in the superstructure construction. Before and aft of the bridge the superstructure is mainly of glass fibre laminate but on *Orpheus* it was of light alloy aluminium. *Ocelot* was the last warship to be built for the Royal Navy at the dockyard at Chatham. She served with the Home Fleet and did some foreign commissions and was finally paid off in 1991 and taken in hand to be preserved and now is part of the Historic Dockyard display and is open for visitors at Chatham.

For details see Page 84, Plate 87, HMS *Onyx* is a sister ship to *Ocelot* and therefore the same in respect of her dimensions and details.

HMS *CHRYSANTHEMUM*

Chrysanthemum is a sloop of the Anchusa (Flower) class, built by Armstrong and launched on 10th November 1917.

Technical specifications:

Of 1,345 tonnes, 262.25 x 35 x 11ft with three x 2 pounders and one MG. Her machinery was four cylinder triple expansion with one screw and two cylindrical boilers. 2,500 SHP = sixteen-and-a-half knots. Coal-fired of 260 tonnes. Complement of ninety-five men. She was briefly used on convoy work in the First World War and then transferred to the Fleet Target Service. Laid off in 1937, she became an RNVR drill ship in 1939 and is moored alongside the Thames embankment in London.

Plate 105 – *HMS* Chrysanthemum *on left side of the photo. (Author's collection.)*

HMS PRESIDENT

A sister ship to *Chrysanthemum*, she was built and launched by Lobritz and Co. Ltd of Renfrew in January 1918, so saw little war service but was built for convoy duties. She now (like *Chrysanthemum*) wears the colours of the Victorian Navy: a black hull with white superstructure and buff funnel. In 1922, she was designated as an RNVR training ship and moored where she is now, astern of HMS *Chrysanthemum* on the Thames embankment, London. Her current use is designated as 'Commercial trade'.

Plate 105 – HMS President *on right side of the photo. (Author's collection.)*

HMS WELLINGTON

Wellington was named out of courtesy for New Zealand where it was originally intended that she would serve. She is a sloop of 990 tonnes and was launched on 29th May 1934 at Devonport dockyard, Plymouth, where she was built. Dimensions of 250 x 36 x 11ft with two x 4.7" and one x 3" guns. She is a Grimsby class of sloop and is the last remaining one to survive of this class. She served on the South Pacific Station until 1939 and spent most of the Second World War years escorting convoys in the North Atlantic and West Africa areas. She took part in the evacuation at Dunkirk and also 'Operation Torch' when the Allies landed in North Africa. Sold off in 1947, she was purchased by the Worshipful Company of Master Mariners and had her engines removed and extensive interior alterations and was then painted white with a buff funnel. She had an extensive refit in 2005 and since then has been awarded a World Ship Trust Award for her very fine preservation. She is now moored near to the other two ships on the Thames embankment.

106

Plate 106 – HMS Wellington *(Author's collection).*

HMS *GANNET*

HMS *Gannet* is a Victorian warship that was one of the early pioneers of composite ships using steam and sail. She was laid down as a Sloop at Sheerness dockyard on the Medway River on 31st August 1878.

Gannet is of the Osprey / Doterel class of Sloops and was ordered on 14th February 1876 at Sheerness Dockyard. Laid down in December 1876, and launched on 31st August 1878, she was commissioned for the first time on 17th April 1879. She is of teak planking on an iron frame and used both sail and steam. Her first commission was on the Pacific Station, between 17th April 1879 and 20th July 1883. During this commission she sailed over 60,000 miles. She returned to Sheerness to pay off. In 1885, following a two-year refit, she sailed for the Mediterranean Station and was there from September 1885 to 1st November 1888. Whilst undergoing a mid-commission refit, she relieved HMS *Dolphin* at Suakin on 11th September 1888 and on the 17th she opened fire with her Poop deck 5' guns in support of the land forces. During the following twenty-seven days, she fired over 200 shells and her machine guns fired nearly 1,200 rounds. HMS *Starling* relieved *Gannet* on 15th October 1888. Her third commission was still in the Med, and she re-commissioned at Malta on 10th November 1888. She then spent three years on survey work before being paid off in December 1891. Her fourth and final commission was again in the Med, from January 1892, and she was then paid off on 16th March 1895 at Chatham. She remained out of commission for four months before being moved to Sheerness Dockyard. In December 1895, she was transferred to the Harbour Service List and returned to Chatham the following June, where she remained until 1900, when she was placed on the list of non-effective vessels. She was an accommodation hulk at The Isle of Grain from October 1900 to June 1902, leased to the South Eastern & Chatham Railway Company. She operated as an accommodation hulk at the cross channel railway terminal at Port Victoria on the Isle of Grain. She then took over from HMS *President* as the drill ship and was moved to West India Docks in the Port of London and underwent major conversions to convert her into a drill ship. Renamed as HMS *President* she became headquarters ship of the London Royal Naval Reserve in June 1903 and, in the spring of 1911, she was replaced as the HQ ship by HMS *Buzzard*.

In 1913 she was lent to Mr C. B. Fry (the cricketer) for use as an accommodation ship for the training school, Mercury. She was towed to Portsmouth by the Battleship, HMS *Queen*. From Portsmouth, she was taken by tug to the River Hamble near Southampton to become the dormitory ship to replace the small *Barque Illova* which had been converted, and was there renamed *Mercury* by the school's founder, Charles Hoare. The Mercury regime was tough and brutal and the boys slept on *Gannet* in hammocks (a most comfortable sleep as the author found out in the Navy). *Mercury* was finally closed down in July 1968 and she was passed back to the Navy, from whom she had been on loan for nearly sixty years, and she was stripped down and moved to Portsmouth as a hulk where she lay (see Plates 109–111) until it was decided to restore her to her former glory. In 1971, her ownership was then transferred by the Navy to The Maritime Trust, who took her in hand to restore her. In 1987, The Chatham Historic Dockyard chartered *Gannet* from the Trust and she was moved to Chatham. In 1994, ownership of *Gannet* was passed over to The Chatham Historic Dockyard Trust. This is a fully credited museum and registered as a charity No. 292101.

Technical specifications:

Of 1,130 tonnes, 170 x 36ft, 2 x 7" and four x 64 pounder guns. Her hull was constructed of teak planking on a steel frame. She undertook slave suppression patrols in the Red Sea between 1885 and 1888 when she stopped Arab slave traders operating off the east coast of Africa, around the Gulf and into the Indian Ocean. She continued doing this work until 16th May 1903 when she was renamed *President* and became a sail and steam training ship. She continued in this role until October 1913 when she was lent out and became the boy's training ship, *Mercury*. She carried on in this role, training very many boys who lived aboard her and who normally joined the Navy as boy seamen, second class. Finally, when boys' training in the Royal Navy was phased out and stopped, there was no longer any need for her and she was then returned to the Navy. She lay idle in Portsmouth harbour for some time (see Plate 107) and then it was decided to rebuild her, but first she had all her superstructure rooms removed and then gutted and she again lay in the harbour waiting to be moved (see Plates 109 and 110). Finally, she was towed to Chatham dockyard and the move of rebuilding her was started. She underwent a £3 million restoration programme and has now been completely rebuilt to the way that she was in 1887. She is a great credit to all the members of the Historic Dockyard at Chatham where she now lies.

Contact:

The Historic Dockyard, Chatham, Kent, ME4 4TZ. England.
Telephone: 44 (0) 1634 823807. Trust Office: 44 (0) 1634 823800. Fax: 44 (0) 1634 823801.
Website: http://www.chdt.org.uk/netsiteCMS/pageid/658/hmsgannet.html

107

Plate 107 – Author's collection.
Plate 108 – Photo courtesy of Navy News and Chatham Historic Dockyard.
Plate 109 – Author's collection.
Plate 110 – Author's collection.
Plate 111 – HMS Gannet at Portsmouth (Author's collection).

MGB 81 *(MTB 416)*

This vessel was built by British Power Boats Ltd at Hythe, Hants, England, and launched on 26th June 1942.

Technical specifications:

71.5ft long x 20.5ft beam x 5.25ft draught. Carried 2,733 gallons fuel, mahogany hard chined, double diagonal sides and triple diagonal on bottom. Speed forty knots, range about 500 miles, with triple Packard engines with three screws. Ninety-six were built for the Navy. Crew of two officers and up to twelve men. One 2 pounder pom pom, one twin Oerlikon and two Lewis guns on pedestals. Two depth charges aft. She saw a lot of service in the Channel and was damaged with one of her crew being killed. She was renumbered as *MTB 416* in September 1943. She was sold off at the end of the War, and was arrested at Shoreham in Sussex for smuggling. She was then sold by the Admiralty and had her engines removed, then resold and turned into a houseboat, then on 24th September 1999 she was reconstructed by the British Military Powerboat Trust Construction at Husband's shipyard at Marchwood, Hants and re-launched on 6th September 2002. She is shown at high speed on trials. Her full war history and other details of the boats saved by these dedicated people can be obtained; see Page 110 for full details of the very interesting book that they have had published. My sincere thanks to Philip Simons for his help.

Plate 112 – MGB 81 *MCA Coastguard Agency. (Photo courtesy of Philip Simons' Collection.)*

Plate 113 – MGB 81 *MCA Coastguard Agency. (Photo courtesy of Philip Simons' Collection.)*

ML 162

This Fairmile 'B' Launch served in the War and shot down six enemy aircraft and was also involved in the sinking of a submarine, and was also at Normandy. At War's end she was transferred to the Dutch Navy and then sold off in 1952 and became the 'Golden Galleon', serving the tourists on the East Anglian coast and The Broads. She now lies, very badly neglected, at Reedham in the Norfolk Broads, and needs some TLC from someone to love and save her.

Contact:

Diane Moffatt, at the Broads Authority Navigation, Reedham, Norfolk.

Plate 114 – ML162 *in her wartime role. (Photo courtesy of Diane Moffatt.)*
Plate 115 – ML162 *(Photo courtesy of Diane Moffatt.)*
Plate 116 – ML162 *(Photo courtesy of Navy News.)*

HMS *BRAVE BORDERER* (P1011)

This boat was one of a class of two. They were the first gas turbine boats built for the Royal Navy by Vospers, of 114 tonnes full load, 90 x 25.5 x 7ft. As MGB 2 x 20mm guns and 2 x 21" TT. Three x Bristol Proteus gas turbines x three shafts. Fuel twenty-five tonnes, fifty-two knots. Three officers and seventeen ratings. In reserve by 1973 and then sold off to civilian interest. Plate 118 shows her at Portsmouth under civilian ownership at the old Gunwharf where she is normally berthed and maintained.

Plate 117 – HMS Brave Borderer *(Author's
collection).*
Plate 118 – HMS Brave Borderer *(Photo
courtesy of Crown).*

H.M.S. BRAVE BORDERER

MTB 467

This Power Boat MTB was built at Hythe, Hants. Launched on 25th March 1944, she
was completed on 18th April 1944 and commissioned the same day. She saw good war
service, sinking two enemy ships with two men killed aboard her. She was sold off
(tender) in November 1954 and moved to a houseboat site at Portsmouth. Finally, the
owner (the author) moved her to Hayling Island when that site was closed down. My
son was born aboard her, so perhaps that makes up for the loss of life on her. She is
still at Hayling as per the Plate 119. Alongside her is another boat from the Portsmouth
site, which was a Free French Air Sea Rescue boat, no. Cinquante (fifty-four) but which

SHOREHAM HOUSEBOATS

There are several more ex-wartime small craft warships that are preserved and used as houseboats at the site in Shoreham, Sussex as follows: MGBs eight, British Power Boats (RN). 120 later MTB 439. BPB. (RN) 137 later MTB 436 BPB (RN) 162 later MTB 481 BPB (RN). 168 BPB later MTB 487 (RN). CMB 104MT (1922) (RN). MTBs 52, 390, Vosper (RN) 426 Whites of Cowes (RN) 490 BPB (RN) 523 BPB (RN) 535 Vosper (RN) RAF HSL 2618, General Service Pinnace GS2 RAF. 2 HS target towing boats RASC Army names 'Kemmel' and 'Raglan'. 2 RAF HSLs, one is No. 186 RAF. 1 MASB (RN) No. unknown. 1 LCI(S) 508 (RN) and two wooden LCAs. Nos. unknown, also an ex-Federal German minesweeper M1096.

Plate 119 – Author's collection.

Plate 120 – Views of the houseboat site at Shoreham. (Photos copyright of Nick Hall.)

Plate 121 – Views of the houseboat site at Shoreham. (Photos copyright of Nick Hall.)

Plate 122 – Views of the houseboat site at Shoreham. (Photos copyright of Nick Hall.)

There are also many more wartime small craft preserved at sites all over the UK but, sadly, due to age, they are decreasing by deterioration. Also, some have been preserved and are in running order and others are just preserved. The following craft are those that have been preserved.

CMB 4 (MTB)

Preserved at Duxford, Cambridgeshire, UK. Length: 39.96 ft, breadth: 8.49ft, displacement: four tonnes. Builder: Thornycroft, Hampton 1916.

Plate 123 – CMB 4. *(Copyright courtesy of National Historic Ships.)*

In 1915, three Naval Lieutenants, Hampden, Anson and Bremner, thought up the idea of a fast attack craft, to have fast hit and run capabilities and be able to skim over minefields to attack German ships in the Heligoland Bight. They would be carried to within sixty miles of their targets by other ships and then launched. They had to be able to do about thirty knots and displace about 4.5 tonnes. Thornycroft had already been experimenting with skimming hulls and had built a class called 'Mirandas'. These were the prototype of the CMBs and they eventually built 117 of them; thirty-nine of the 40ft class and seventy-three of the later 55ft class, and five minelayers. The bases were in Osea Island on the Blackwater River and in Essex and Dunkirk. The Dunkirk boats claimed four sinkings. The small class carried one torpedo and the larger class carried two. They were carried pointing ahead in a recess on the stern, and launched by pushing them over the stern, on rails, by a steel ram. As the torpedo was a lot faster then their boat, the CMB had to swerve sharply out of the danger of its own torpedo. CMB 4 is a 40ft type boat in which Lt Agar won the VC when he sank a Russian ship in Konstaft in 1919. This one is preserved on a cradle, indoors at Duxford by the Imperial War Museum. It is probably the only one left. A later model of this boat is CMB MTB 331, which was built in 1939 and is now stored at Upper Heyford Museum and the Vosper 60ft MTB 71 is also now at the Duxford collection. The privately owned MTB 102, like MGB 81 (Plate 112) is still used under her own power after being restored. A lot of boats were restored and preserved at the British Military Powerboat Trust at Marchwood in Hampshire, UK, but this has now closed down and the boats have been dispersed.

Contact:

Website: http://duxford.iwm.org.uk/

MTB 331

Type: 55ft CMBT. Service: Royal Navy. Builder: Thornycroft, Hampton. Year built: 1941. Number built: fourteen. Displacement: seventeen tonnes. Dimensions: length: 55ft, beam: 11½ft, draught: 4ft. Hull: mahogany. Engines: 2 x 650 HP Thornycroft. Maximum speed: forty knots.

A Mr Morley appears to have taken *MTB 331* in hand for restoration and also got the late Commander, Peter Thornycroft, who was then connected with TT Boat designs Ltd, Benbridge, Isle of Wight, in his plans for *MTB 331's* restoration. He arranged for *Jonrey* (as she was then known) to be transported by road to Moody's Boat Yard and then taken over to Cowes, Isle of Wight, where all the equipment that had been added to her to make her into a cabin cruiser was removed. In September 1981, *MTB 331* was on chocks at Shepards Wharf, Cowes; her old superstructure had been removed and Harmo Thornycroft, Peter's son, had stripped off the many coats of paint that covered her, down to the original hull planking. She was then towed over from Cowes to the former Royal Naval Armament depot (RNAD) at Priddy's Hard to their museum's store adjoining Chilcombe House, Chilcombe Lane, Winchester, where the Hampshire County Council Museum Services collection of historic Thornycroft vehicles and memorabilia was housed. In April of 1992, *MTB 331* was moved from Chilcombe House to Maritime Workshops Ltd, Ferrol Rd, Gosport, for conservation work (thought to have cost about £75,000) which commenced in 1992. Following this period of restoration, *MTB331* was displayed at the 'Dockyard 500' exhibition held at Portsmouth Naval Base in June 1995. Later, she was again moved back to Priddy's Hard where she was stored and then transported by road to BMPT at Marchwood in March 2000. She was put on show at the IFOS at Portsmouth in 2001.

Plate 124 – *55ft Coastal Motor Torpedo Boat. (Photo copyright of British Military Powerboat Trust.)*

Plate 125 – Jonrey *at Priddy's Hard, 1981. (Photo copyright of British Military Powerboat Trust.)*

Plate 126 – Jonrey *at Teignmouth. (Photo copyright of British Military Powerboat Trust.)*

MTB331 is now owned by Hampshire County Council UK and is the sole survivor of her class. She has been fully restored and is now a seagoing craft which can be seen at all types of nautical shows in England.

For further reading on the preservation of small craft in the UK, the following publications are available: 'A Guide to the Military Small Craft at Marchwood,' 'RAF Marine Craft Directories,' and 'Retired on the River'.

Contact:
25 Greenways, Highlands Rd, Portslade, Brighton, BN41 2BS, England.

HMS *IVESTON*

This 'Ton' class minesweeper (M1151) is of the same class as *Bronington* on Page 86. She has been bought by the Thurrock Sea Cadet Corps unit and is now used as a training ship. She is moored at Thurrock (UK). Built by Philip and Son, Dartmouth, she was laid down on 22nd October 1952, launched on 1st June 1954, and was in service on 20th June 1955.

Technical specifications: (and those of *Bronington*):

Displacement (full load) 370 tonnes, speed fifteen knots (cruising). Dimensions: 46.33 x 8.76 x 2.50ft. Armed with one x 40mm mk7 AA. Radar and sonar. M2 x Paxman Deltic 18A-7A diesels, two props: 3,000 HP. Fuel: forty-three tonnes. Range 3,000/8; 2,300/13. Crew: five officers and thirty-three men.

TS *NELSON*

At Norwich (England) is the TS *Nelson*, a Sea Cadet training ship that was the Swedish Minelayer HSwMS *Vale* (P155). She was de-commissioned in 1995 and sold to the Cadet Corps for £30,000 and it cost them £93,000 to refurbish her and convert her to a training ship. It is to be presumed that her engines have been removed. She was one of seventeen of the Hugin Class built by Bergens Mekanske Vaksted, of Norway, laid down on 3rd October 1978, and in service by 26th April 1979.

Technical specifications:

(As she was Swedish dimensions appear in Swedish metric.)

Of 120 tonnes, speed thirty-five knots. Dimensions: 36.53 x 6.20 x 1.60 metres, two x 6 Penguin Mk 32 (1 x 6), 1 x 57mm Bofor and carried twenty-four mines.

May she serve the Sea Cadets faithfully.

MTB 102, which is a Vosper experimental boat built in 1937, was sold off at War's end and then became a houseboat at Portchester Castle (Hampshire). She was eventually bought by the Power Boats Trust and re-converted back to her original configuration. She displaced thirty-two tonnes, with dimensions of 67.25 x 14.5 x 3.25ft. Three shafts, Isotta-Franschini petrol BHP 3,450 motors = 43.75 knots. One x 20mm gun and two x 21" TT. She is now fully operational and is normally based at Southampton (Hampshire). She was used in the feature film 'Fooling Hitler' when she was shown offshore twice as she was in the Second World War.

Based in Plymouth (Devon) is the ex-*ML 293* which is a Fairmile 'B' class. More details of this vessel would be appreciated.

SCHNELLBOOT (S 130), (P5230)

Being restored and preserved at Torpoint, Devon, UK, is the ex *Kreigsmarine Schnellboot S130*; these boats were called 'E' boats by the Allies. This boat is the sole survivor of this class of boat and was used in the North Sea and the Channel in 1943–45 and was one of the attacking boats against the American Exercise 'Tiger' D-Day rehearsal at Slapton Sands, Devon, where many US servicemen died when attacked by these boats. She was captured at the end of the War by the British and renumbered *P5230*, disarmed to be fitted with cameras and then went out to gather intelligence on the Russians. Later these boats were used, under the White Ensign, to insert agents into the Soviet-occupied Baltic States, under the banner of the 'British Baltic Fishery Protection Service'. The group was disbanded and the boats were handed over to the West German Bundesmarine. Finally she was paid off in 1991 and sold off to be converted into a houseboat, as were many others at War's end. The author knows of two on the houseboat site where his boat was moored at Portsmouth, but both of them were broken up for scrap. She was then bought for restoration by a military collector, Kevin Wheatcroft, who owns some 200 plus vintage military vehicles. He has put her to be preserved and made seaworthy again at Torpoint, Devon.

Contact:

The Wheatcroft collection, The Farm, Lutterworth Road, Arnesby, Leicestershire, LE8 5UT, England.

E-mail: orinfo@s130.co.uk

Website: oratwww.s130.co.uk

127

Plates 127, 128 and 129 – Schnellboot S130 *(Photos courtesy of Kevin Wheatcroft.)*

At the British Military Powerboat Trust facility at Marchwood, Hampshire, UK, are the following ex-Coastal Forces boats, which are either undergoing preservation, or are preserved there:

HSL 102 (High Speed Launch) 64ft boat, built by British Power Boats in 1936, owned by Powerboat restorations.

HSL 142 (as above), built in 1941, owned by Mick Dent.

ST 206 37.5ft ST (as above) built in 1931, owned by Powerboat Restorations.

ST 1502 41.5ft ST (as above) built in 1942, owned by BMPT.

ST 1510 (as above) built in 1942, owned by Mr John Hessletine.

TARGET BOAT 35ft, fast motor boat, in 1940, owned by BMPT.

MTB 71 60ft MTB, built by Vosper in 1940, owned by Hampshire County Council.

The book *The Houseboats of Sussex, Hampshire and Dorset* by Philip Simons details other coastal *MGB*s and *MTB*s that have been preserved, for those who wish to follow this line of preservation. It is available from Small Craft Group Publications, 5 Rogate Drive, Thornbury, Plymouth, UK. PL6 8SY.

Contact:

aiholtham@virginmeadia.com

HM ROYAL YACHT BRITANNIA

Though not officially designated as a warship, *Britannia* was a Fleet vessel of the Royal Navy and was manned by serving sailors and Royal Marines and carried an Admiral when at sea. Her pendant number was A00, which designates an auxiliary vessel in the Fleet and the numbers 00 put her ahead of all the other auxiliaries. She also had two x3 pounder guns, although these were only used for saluting purposes.

Technical specifications:

Her details are 3,990 tonnes, 4,961 full load, 5,769 gross. Built by John Brown's shipyard at Clydebank and laid down in February 1952, she was launched on 16th April 1953 and entered service on 14th January 1954. Dimensions are 380w, 412.2 overall, beam 55ft, draught 15.6 mean at load, 17 max. Main engines are single reduction geared steam turbines with two shafts; 12,000 SHP = twenty-one knots approximately cruising speed. Did 22.75 on trials. Two boilers. Fuel 550 tonnes (max). Radius was 2,100 at twenty knots, 2,400 at eighteen and 3,000 at fifteen knots. Complement was 271 officers and men. She was designed as a hospital ship but in peacetime was to be used as the Queen's Royal Yacht. The bridge and funnel are built of aluminium. She was fitted with Denny Brown single fin stabilisers to reduce her rolling from twenty degrees to six degrees in bad weather. She cost £2,980,000 to build. In 1958, the top twenty feet of her mainmast and the wireless aerial on her foremast were hinged so that they could be lowered if needed to pass under low bridges. She was equipped with 2/1006 radar.

As a hospital ship she would have 200 beds and 60 medical personnel and be fitted with a helicopter platform. During her 1980 last refit, she was re-boilered at a cost of £2.1 million, which brought her total cost over her active life to £12 million. She was equipped to burn distillate fuel in 1984, which made her unsuitable to go to the Falklands conflict as a hospital ship because she would have been the only ship there to use this fuel.

She was eventually paid off and into reserve but then put up for sale and purchased by a consortium for civilian use. They overhauled her and she is now moored at the Ocean Terminal at Leith near Edinburgh in the UK and has been converted into a floating restaurant.

The Monitor on display in the Dockyard at Portsmouth in a basin has been re-painted in her original wartime dazzle colours.

Plate 130 – Britannia *Moored at Ocean Terminal, Leith. Photo courtesy of Ian A White.*
Plate 131 – Britannia *Moored at Ocean Terminal, Leith. Photo courtesy of Ian A White.*

PART THREE
AUSTRALIA

HMAS *VAMPIRE* (No. 11)

Vampire is built to the specifications of the British Daring class, but was built at Cockatoo Island Dockyard, Sydney. Laid down on 1st July 1952, launched on 27th October 1956 and completed on 23rd June 1958, she is one of a class of three, the most notable being *Voyager,* which was lost in a collision with the Aircraft carrier, *Melbourne.*

Technical specifications:

(Dimensions shown in Australian metric)

Her displacement is 2,800 tonnes, 3,600 full load, length 366m x beam 13.4m x draught 3.9m. Guns 6 x 4.5", 6 x 40 mm AA. One x 3 barrelled Limbo DC mortar. Boilers were Foster Wheeler 650psi, English Electric geared turbines, two shafts, 54,000 SHP. Speed = 30.5 knots. Range 3,700 miles at twenty knots. Oil fuel 584 tonnes, crew of fourteen officers and 306 ratings. Her superstructure is of light alloy, not steel, to save weight. In 1971 she and her sister ships were refitted at a cost of $A11 million. This included the fitting of Mark Twenty-two fire control systems, new air warning and navigation radars, modernised communications, enclosed bridge, modernized turrets and new funnels. *Duchess* was lent from the Royal Navy for four years on 8th May 1964, extended to 1971 to replace *Voyager* and was then purchased by the RAN in 1972. They were the largest destroyers ever to be built in Australia. When finally laid off, she was purchased by the Sydney Maritime Museum where she is now moored.

Contact:

Australian National Maritime Museum, 2 Murray Street, Darling Harbour, Sydney, NSW 2000, Australia.

Plate 132 – *HMAS* Vampire *Author's collection.*

HMAS *ONSLOW* (S60)

Also moored at the Sydney Museum site, alongside *Vampire,* is the Australian submarine *Onslow.* Of the British 'Oberon' class, she is one of six that were bought by the RAN. Built by Scott's SB Engineering of Greenock, Scotland, she was laid down on 26th May 1967, launched on 29th August 1968 and was in service by 22nd December 1969.

Technical specifications:

(Dimensions shown in Australian metric)

Displacement of up to 2,417 tonnes, speed fifteen knots. Length 89.9m x 8.07 x 5.48. Six tubes for sub Harpoon and US Mk48 Mod. Three torpedoes with twelve reloads. 2 x 3 x 3,680 HP. Admiralty standard range sixteen VVs-ASR1 diesel engines, and diesel-electric propulsion, 6,000 HP. Radar 1/1006 and Sonar 1/187 C 'Micro Puffs'. Complement six officers and fifty-seven men. All six of this class received mid-life modernisation, *Onslow* from August 1982 to December 1984. Upon receiving the new class of submarine being delivered, these boats were eventually laid off to Reserve and *Onslow* was bought by the Sydney Maritime Museum to be placed alongside *Vampire.* Also of this class is HMAS *Ovens* S70 preserved at Fremantle (see Pages 116–117 Plates 135 and 136) and *Oxley* S57 was scrapped on the shiplift at Henderson, Cockburn Sound WA. (See Page 117, Plates 137 and 138).

HMAS *Otway* is preserved at Holbrook, NSW, Australia.

HMAS *ADVANCE*

Also at the Sydney Museum is *Advance*, one of twenty-one 'Attack' class patrol boats which have been superseded by the Fremantle class. She was laid down at Walkers yard in March 1967, launched on 16th August 1967 and was in service by 24th January 1968. She displaces 146 tonnes and is 32.76 x 6.2 x 1.9 metres with 1 x 40mm AA Mark 7, 2 x 7.62 MGs and Decca Radar. Two Davey Paxman Ventura 16 YJCM diesels x two props: 3,500 HP. Range 1,220/13. Crew: three officers and nineteen ratings. Steel hull with light alloy superstructure. Some went to Papua New Guinea and some to Indonesia. She is the last one left of her class in Australian waters.

(Dimensions shown in Australian metric)

Plate 133 – HMAS Advance. *Author's collection.*

THE *KRAIT*

Though not strictly a warship, the *Krait* is also preserved at Sydney. She was used by Australian SAS men to land them at Singapore during the Second World War to attack shipping there and after the end of the War was taken in hand for preservation. The plaque states 'Australian WW2 Raider built as a Japanese fishing boat. Built 1930s.'

Contact:

Australian National Maritime Museum, 2 Murray Street, Darling Harbour, Sydney, NSW 2000, Australia. GPO Box 5131, Sydney, NSW, Australia.

Telephone: 02 9298 3777 – Fax: 02 9298 3660.

Website: www.anmm.gov.au

Plate 134 – *The* Krait. *(Author's collection.)*
Plate 135 – *HMAS* Ovens *S70. (Author's collection.)*

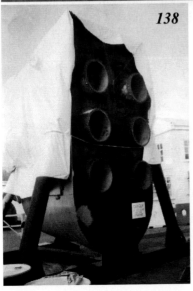

Plate 136 – HMAS Ovens S70 on the slipway at Fremantle, at the Fremantle Maritime Museum. For details of this boat, see HMAS Onslow Page 114 (Photo courtesy of Author's collection.)

Plate 137 – HMAS Oxley S57. At Jervoise Bay, Cockburn Sound, being scrapped April 1992. (Photo courtesy of Author's collection.)

Plate 138 – The bow torpedo tubes salvaged from the scrapped HMAS Oxley S57, now preserved at the Fremantle Maritime Museum. (Photo courtesy of Author's collection.)

HMAS *DIAMANTINA* (K377) later (GOR 377)

Diamantina is a River class frigate, one of a class of sixteen ships which were designed in Britain but built in Australia. She was used as an anti-submarine ship. Seven sister ships were built in Australia, but by 1984 only eight were still in service and she is the only survivor of the class in Australia. Named after a river in Queensland, which was named after the wife of the first Governor of the State. Built by Walkers of Maryborough she was laid down on 12th April 1943, launched on 6th April 1944 and commissioned on 27th April 1945.

Technical specifications:

Of 2,220 tonnes full load, she is 301ft x 36.6ft x 12ft draught. She has two x 4 cylinder triple expansion stream engines of 5,500 IHP. Two water tube boilers, twin screw, speed 19/20 knots. She has two x 4" H.A. guns, three Bofors, 40mm AA and ten x 20mm Oerlikon AA. She served in the New Guinea and Solomons area during the later part of the Second World War and the Japanese surrender at Nauru was signed on her. Paid off to reserve, she was reactivated on 2nd June 1959 as an Oceanic research ship and worked out of Fremantle. The author had the pleasure of doing two refits on her at the slipway (where the Submarine *Ovens* is now) and when you go down the ladder into the engine room, if you look at the fire main in front of you, you will notice that it has a spool piece with flanges in it, and I did that when the fire main developed a leak whilst under refit. Her engines were in good condition when we repaired them. She was laid up at Sydney in January 1980 for disposal. In 1980 she was presented to the QMMA and steamed to Brisbane in October and put in a dry dock there. The dry dock has since flooded and she is now floating. She has been returned to her wartime configuration. It is hoped to raise the funds to repair the dry dock so that she can be out of the water again to help preserve her.

139

Plate 139 – Diamantina *in her dry dock at Brisbane. (Photo courtesy of Author's collection.)*

Plate 140 – Diamantina *in her dry dock at Brisbane. (Photo courtesy of Author's collection.)*

HMAS *CASTLEMAIN*

HMAS *Castlemain* is one of the numerous Bathurst class of Fleet minesweepers (very often referred to as Corvettes, which they were not) of fifty-two ships which were all built by Australian shipyards to a design that was based on the British Bangor class. She was launched on 7th August 1941 and went into service at once.

Technical specifications:

Displacement: 733 tonnes (938 at full load). Complement: seventy men. Dimensions: 186 x 31 x 8.5ft (mean draught). Guns one x 3" (4" on some). One x 20mm Oerlikon, four mg. Machinery: two shafts triple expansion. IHP 1,800 = sixteen knots. The war losses were HMAS *Armidale*, *Geelong* and *Wallaroo*.

Several of this class were sold to other Navies, namely four to the Royal Indian Navy, eight to the Royal Netherlands Navy and five to the Turkish Navy. Three of the class were war losses and another hit a mine and sank off the Queensland coast on 13th September 1947. They were a sturdy class of ship and good seaworthy vessels, well liked by their crews. She saw sterling war service and was finally taken from the active list and by 1955 was a static training ship, allocated to HMAS *Cerberus* for engine room personnel training. She was towed from Geelong where she was laid up to Williamstown dockyard, where she had a complete engine overhaul and all other non-essential equipment was removed from her. She was so used as a training ship for fifteen years and by 1969 she was declared 'as for disposal' and by then she was a badly rusting vessel in a pitiful condition. She was finally offered for 'sale by tender as lying' with tenders closing by 24th June 1971. It seems that someone had a soft heart for, when the Navy was approached, they finally decided to gift her to the Maritime Trust of Australia (an organisation that does sterling work to preserve old ships). When they took possession of her she was in a terrible state, rusting and gutted out of all her fittings with the engines dissembled and in pieces. It was found that the engines could not be reassembled to take her to Melbourne so she was to be towed there. In February 1974 a team of volunteers was assembled and she was towed to berth No. 7 at South Wharf where the Melbourne Harbour Trust Commissioners had very kindly offered the use of this berth. Over the years, she has been readily restored by hard working people to her original condition by the use of parts from other ships that were being scrapped in Australia and New Zealand. She is now a beautifully restored vessel and a credit to her restorers and is berthed at Gem Pier, Williamstown, Victoria and is open for public inspection.

Contact:

PO Box 244, Williamstown, Victoria 3016.
Telephone: (03) 9397 2363 weekends or (03) 9853 0823 before 10 a.m. weekdays.
Website: http://www.hmascastlemaine.com/page1.htm.

She is well worth a visit to see what the smaller classes of ships in the Navy were like to live and serve in. The author has served on small ships and enjoyed the informality better than the regimentation of 'big ships'.

141

photo courtesy of Maritime Trust of Australia.

HMAS Castlemaine

Australian World War 2 Minesweeper.
On display at Williamstown, Melbourne

World War 2 Minesweeper

OPEN FOR
INSPECTION

Plate 141 – Photo courtesy of Maritime Trust of Australia.

HMAS *WHYALLA* (J153)

Type: A/S and M/S Vessel, Bathurst Class, built to the design of the British 'Bangor' Class. A total of sixty corvettes were built in Australia – thirty-six for RAN, twenty for RN and four for RTN. Four of them were constructed in BHP *Whyalla* for RAN.

Technical specifications:

(Dimensions shown in Australian metric)

Displacement: 650 tonnes, length: 56.73m, beam: 9.44m, depth: 4.72m, speed: fifteen knots (design), 12.9 (trial). Engines: T.K. Triple expansions. Boilers: two Yarrow type, oil fired.

Wartime colour: Keel to top of boot topping grey (prior to 1944), black (after 1944). Keel above boot topping grey, decks light grey, forecastle deck dark grey, mine sweeping deck dark grey, funnel grey. A crew of eighty-five.

Armament:

4" calibre, cartridge, Mark IV, produced at the Royal Naval Gun Factory (UK) in 1918. Maximum range eight miles. The shell weighed 25lb; loading case 16lb. Ammunition used included High Explosive, Semi-Armour Piercing, Starshell, Shrapnel and Common Purpose shells. Two 20mm Oerlikon anti-aircraft guns and one 40mm Bofors anti-aircraft gun.

Depth charges: search and defence. Surface and aerial radar (detection of ships and aircraft), retractable sonar (ASDIC) – detection of submarines.

Construction:

Keel laid on 24th July 1940. Launched by Lady Muriel Barclay-Harvey (wife of the South Australian Governor) on 12th May 1941. Commissioned on 8th January 1942. She was the first modern warship to be built in South Australia.

Service:

Since the declaration of the Second World War, German and later Japanese submarines became active along the southern and eastern coasts of Australia, attacking Australian and allied merchantmen convoys. By the end of 1941, more than seventy German mines had been discovered off Spencer Gulf, Hobart, Bass Strait and the NSW coast between Sydney and Newcastle.

HMAS *Whyalla* was anchored in Sydney Harbour on 31st May 1942 when the Japanese midget submarines attack took place.

In January 1943, HMAS *Whyalla* became the first RAN warship to participate in the survey of unknown coastal waters of Papua New Guinea. In the same month, while in a deep inlet on Cape Nelson Peninsula, she was attacked by eighteen Japanese dive bombers and six fighters. Two Oerlikon AA gun crew were wounded and one Japanese fighter was shot down at the sea level. No damage to the ship.

At Milne Bay she ran aground on a coral reef while conducting a survey. As a later result of this particular survey, Milne Bay became a major Allied base during the US offensive in the south west Pacific in 1943.

In April 1943, Milne Bay was raided by Japanese bombers. HMAS *Whyalla* rendered great assistance to allied ships in escaping manoeuvres.

In November 1943, HMAS *Whyalla* resumed escort duties off the east coast of Australia.

In December 1944, she was engaged in mine sweeping operations off the south east coast of Australia. On 28th December 1944, off Cape Everard, a whale rose under the forefoot of the ship and collided with the A/S sonar dome. The A/S was immediately out of action and the oscillator missing. The whale survived.

In 1945, HMAS *Whyalla* was attached to the British Pacific Fleet and formed part of the occupying forces that received the Japanese surrender of Hong Kong. She was paid off into reserve on 16th May 1946 after steaming over 110,000 nautical miles during her wartime career. In February 1947 she was sold to the Victorian Ports and Harbours in Melbourne. The vessel was renamed the *Rip* and serviced pile lights off the Port Phillip Bay and conducted blasting operations on a dangerous rip at the entrance of the Port Phillip Bay until 1984. In 1987, the ship was permanently landlocked in Whyalla and is the largest landlocked museum ship on display in Australia, two miles from the sea.

Contact:

Curator: Paul Mazourek, Whyalla Maritime Museum, Lincoln Highway, Whyalla, South Australia, 5600.

Telephone: (08) 8645 8900 – Fax: (08) 8645 3620. Freecall: 1800 088 589.

E-mail: paulmazourek@whyalla.sa.gov.au

Website: www.maritime.org/hnsa.whyalla.htm

http://www.whyalla.com/site/page.cfm?u=93

Whyalla Museum opening times: 10 a.m. to 4 p.m., seven days a week. Ship tours: April to October: 10 a.m., 11 a.m., noon, 1 p.m., 2 p.m. November to March: 11 a.m., noon, 1 p.m., 2 p.m., 3 p.m.

142

Plate 142 – *The* Whyalla *(Photo courtesy of Richard Humphrys and the* Whyalla *Maritime Museum)*

HMVS (HMAS) *CERBERUS*

Cerberus is a Monitor type battleship and was the first British-built warship to fully dispense with sails and incorporated a shallow draught. She was also the first in the world to have a central superstructure and fore and aft gun turrets, and also the first armoured warship to be built for the Australian (then Victorian) Navy. This turret ship was of 3,344 tonnes, 225 x 45ft with four x 10" guns. Built by the Palmer shipbuilding Company at Jarrow on Tyne and commissioned on 2nd December 1868, she was a trial ship of a group being of a design entirely new to the Navy. She sailed for Australia in October 1870 with a scratch crew of people and some of her crew spent spells in jail at ports of call (Lisbon and Malta); her passage was made at about five knots and she arrived off Williamstown, Victoria, on 9th April 1871. For quite some while she was a conspicuous figure in the Hobson's Bay area and a horse shoerock enclosure was built in a position commanding the entrance to Port Phillip into which the ship could be floated and secured (Pope's Eye Fort), giving her, besides her mobile qualities, a fixed defence unit. As a weapon of offence, she was considered more than a match for the rest of Her Majesty's ships on the station. Her armoured hull and turrets made her too tough a ship for any vessel of her time to beat. In 1910 she was relegated to harbour service and in 1911 she became part of the Royal Australian Navy. She was renamed *Platypus II* and then became a depot ship in 1918. Finally, she was sold off to the Melbourne Salvage Co., her hull was sunk as a breakwater in July 1926. She is now the only Monitor warship left in the world and is the only survivor of Australia's pre-Federation Navies. Her name is carried on to this day by a shore base in Flinders, Victoria.

She now rests in three metres of water in Half Moon Bay and is in a rotting state. A protection order has been placed on her and she is not allowed to be boarded.

Friends of the *Cerberus* intend to raise her from her sunken breakwater resting place and rest her on a submerged supporting structure reckoned to cost about $6.5 million to complete.

Contact details:

Friends of the Cerberus Inc. PO Box 1231, Blackburn North, Victoria, Australia, 3130.

In the museum of Canberra are stored two midget Japanese submarines Nos M22 and 23. These were captured at the end of the War with Japan and shipped to the Australian Canberra Museum where they can still be seen. Also, one, the M24, was sunk in Sydney Harbour and raised in 1945, but details of what happened to this wreck when salvaged are unknown.

Plate 143 – HMVS Cerberus. *(Photo courtesy of the Friends of* Cerberus.*)*
Plate 144 – HMVS Cerberus. *The fore-turret and bridge. The steel plating on top of the turret has only been removed recently. (Photo courtesy of the Friends of* Cerberus.*)*
Plate 145 – HMVS Cerberus. *Looking aft from the bow. The turrets can be rotated to face inwards. Two armoured cupolas can be seen on top of the turret. (Photo courtesy of the Friends of* Cerberus.*)*
Plate 146 – HMVS Cerberus. *As seen from the shore. A harbour light has been fitted on the stern. (Photo courtesy of the Friends of* Cerberus.*)*

143

144

145

146

PART FOUR
REST OF THE WORLD

 CANADA

HMCS *HAIDA* (DD215) ex (G63)

HMCS *Haida* is a destroyer based on the British Tribal class of ships, one of twenty-seven eventually built of which Canada had eight; the others were *Athabaskan* (1) (ex *Iroquois*), *Huron*, *Iroquois* (ex-*Athbaskan*), *Cayuga*, *Micmac*, *Nookta*, and *Athbaskan* (2) *Haida* like the *Huron*, *Athbaskan* (1) and *Iroquois* were built at Vickers Armstrong's yard at Tyneside (UK) and she was launched on 25th August 1942 and commissioned for the first time on 30th August 1943. The others in Canadian service were built at the Halifax shipyard. War loss was *Athbaskan* (1) replaced by *Athbaskan* (2). *Haida* served admirably out of Plymouth (UK) in the Atlantic theatre of war as a part of the 10th Destroyer flotilla, and drove the German *T27* ashore to destruction in April 1944 and she was also involved in the destruction and sinking of the German submarine *U971* on 24th June 1944. She also destroyed fourteen enemy ships in the English Channel and the Bay of Biscay. She took part in two tours of duty in the Korean War and is now the only survivor in the world of this class of ship. Her sister ship, *Athbaskan* (2), sank the German *T29* in action on 26th April 1944.

Technical specifications:

Empty displacement 2,000 tonnes, length 377ft overall, beam 37.5ft, draught 9.6ft. Originally armed with six x 4.7" guns, two x 4" AA, twelve x 20mm Oerlikon AA guns, four torpedo tubes and one rack of depth charges with two depth charge throwers and also one quad 40mm pom pom AA gun, a very formidable armament indeed. Machinery: Parsons geared turbines, two shafts, SHP 44,000 = 36.5 knots. Boilers were three x Admiralty three drum type.

She was finally paid off from Naval service on 11th October 1963 and on 21st September 1964 she was presented to the City of Toronto as a memorial and she lay at the waterfront for thirty-eight years. Finally, in 2002, she was acquired by the Federal Agency Parks, Canada, with a contribution of $5 million to do repairs on her hull and superstructure. In 2003, on the year of her sixtieth anniversary of commissioning, after being dry-docked, she was towed to the City of Hamilton, Ontario where she now lies at peace and beautifully preserved by her carers. She is now rated as a 'Canadian National Historic Site' and long may she remain so.

She is now preserved at Hamilton, Ontario, and is owned by Parks Canada.

His Majesty's Canadian Destroyer *Haida* was commissioned on 31st August 1943, joining her sisters of the Tribal class, the *Athabaskan, Huron* and *Iroquois*, as a part of the Tenth Destroyer Flotilla out of Plymouth, England, along with ships from the Royal Navy and the free Polish Navy.

Other Second World War patrols were in the English Channel and the Bay of Biscay in 1944 where she added several other sinkings to her record. Two tours of duty in the Korean conflict in 1952 and 1953 reinforced her claim to the title of 'The Fightingest Ship in the RCN'.

De-commissioned in September 1963, she was purchased by a group of Ontario businessmen for display as a memorial in Toronto. That group operated her as a tourist attraction until 1970. Since then, the *Haida* has been owned and operated by the Provincial Government of Ontario, the Department of Industry and Tourism, and the Department of National Defence.

Visitors to the *Haida* from 21st May to 14th October each year may view the ship not only as a memorial but also as a working vessel. During those months the ship is used by the Department of National Defence for a service of cadet courses.

Contact:

HMCS Haida National Historic Site, 57 Discovery Drive, Hamilton, Ontario, L8L 8K4, Canada.
Telephone: 905 526 0911.
E-mail: haida.info@pc.gc.ca
Website: www.pc.gc.ca

She is open to the general public from 24th May to 4th September, seven days a week from 10 a.m. to 5 p.m. and four days per week from 4th September to mid-October (Thursdays to Sundays).

She is well worth a visit and is in immaculate condition thanks to her carers so please support her.

The other ships of this class were: British – *Eskimo, Ashanti, Nubian, Tartar*, and the following were lost in action: *Afridi, Bedouin, Cossack* of Altmark fame 'The Navy's here', *Gurkha, Maori, Mashona, Matabele, Mohawk, Punjabi, Sikh, Somali*, and *Zulu*. Australian – *Warramunga, Bataan* (ex-*Kurna*), *Arunta*.

Plates 147 and 148 – HMCS Haida.
(Photo courtesy of Parks Canada)
Plate 149 – HMCS Haida *(1949 R.C.N. Official).*
Plate 150 – HMCS Haida *at war (Photo courtesy of Parks Canada).*
Plate 151 – HMCS Haida *at Hamilton (Photo courtesy of Parks Canada).*

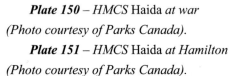

HMCS SACKVILLE (K181)

Sackville is a 'Long Forecastle' Flower class corvette of the Royal Canadian Navy. One of sixty-three ships of this class built for the Canadian Navy, there were 236 altogether built in the UK and Canada. Displacement of 925 tonnes, 1,170 full load, 205ft (overall) x 33 x 14.10ft. Guns one x Mk IX 4"AA x MK VIII 2 pounder on an anti-aircraft mounting, two x 20mm AA, four depth charge throwers and one x Mk 3 hedgehog anti-submarine mortar. Machinery: triple expansion. IHP 2,800 = sixteen knots. Boilers, two Admiralty three drum. She was laid down at St John Shipbuilding and Drydock Co. at St John, New Brunswick, Canada. Launched on 15th May 1941, and commissioned on 30th December 1941. Complement of eighty officers and men. Endurance of 4,000 miles at twelve knots. She is the last corvette left in the world and is preserved and moored at Halifax, Nova Scotia. She spent her operational career escorting convoys between St

John's, Newfoundland and Londonderry, Northern Ireland. On 3rd to 4th August 1942, when escorting one of these convoys eastbound, she engaged three German U Boats in a thirty-six-hour period. In bad weather, Lt Alan Easton and his crew damaged one submarine, hit another with her 4" gun and damaged a third with her depth charges. For this action, Lt Easton was awarded the DSC and his crew were commended for their service. At the end of the War, she was relegated to be an officers' training ship and was eventually paid off into the reserve fleet. She was reactivated for service in 1952 and spent the next thirty years in oceanographic, hydrographic and fisheries research. She was finally paid off from the Navy in 1982 and then transferred to the Canadian Naval Corvette Trust, which has beautifully restored her to her 1944 condition. On 4th May 1985, *Sackville* was formally dedicated as a Canadian Naval Memorial. She is a credit to all her loving carers and a fitting tribute to all those Canadian men who served on her and all the other ships in the Royal Canadian Navy.

Technical specifications:

Displacement: 925 tonnes. Dimensions: 193 (pp), 205 (overall) x 33 x 14½ft. Guns: 1-4 inch AA, several smaller. Machinery: Triple expansion. IHP 2,800 = sixteen knots. Boilers: 2 S.E. in earlier ships, possibly two Admiralty three-drum type in later units.

This 'Flower' class corvette is now restored to her wartime condition and is moored in summer at Halifax harbour and during the winter at the nearby naval dockyard. A request for a photo was ignored.

Contact:

The Canadian Naval Memorial Trust, HMCS *Sackville*, PO Box 99000, Halifax, Nova Scotia, B3K 5X5, Canada.
Telephone: (1 902) 429 2132 (June to October), (1 902) 427 2837 (November to May).
Fax: (1 902) 427 1346.
E-mail: secretary@hmcssackville-cnmt.ns.ca
Website: http://www.hmcssackville-cnmt.ns.ca

Plate 152 – HMCS Sackville *(1943 R.C.N. Official).*
Plate 153 – HMCS Sackville *(photo courtesy of Sandy McClearn).*
Plate 154 – HMCS Sackville *(photo courtesy of Sandy McClearn).*

HMCS *ONONDAGA* (S73)

At Quebec in Canada is the Oberon class submarine HMCS *Onondaga (S73)*. Launched at Chatham Dockyard UK on 25th September 1967 and commissioned 22nd June 2000. Her statistics are the same as the other Oberon classes shown in this book. She is one of three purchased for Canada from the UK during the 1960s to replace their former US submarines which were outdated. She was defined as a 'Super O Boat' and had many differences from the other 'O' boats built which included an open concept control room, an inboard battery ventilation system, a radar room in the machinery space and Canadian built communications systems. In the 1980s all three were upgraded. Her stern tubes were removed, sonar was modernised, and her Mk 37 torpedos were replaced with mark 48s. The fire control systems were also updated. She saw service with the Canadian Fleet for 33 years, and set a new record as this was longer than any other submarine in the Canadian Navy had ever served for. She travelled about 500,000 nautical miles (about half underwater) and visited over 54 ports in eleven countries and also served with NATO. She was laid off and reduced to reserve in 2007 and finally in 2009 joined the Site Historique Maritime de la Pointe-au-Pere museum.

Contact:

1034 du Phare, Rimouski, Quebec, G5M 1L8, Canada.
Telephone: 418 724 6214 – Fax 418 721 0815.
Email: info@shmp.qc.ca/
Website: http://www.shmp.qc.ca/

155

Plate 155 – HMCS Onondaga (S73). (Photo is courtesy of Historic Naval Ships Association for which I thank them.)

RUSSIA

RUSSIAN CRUISER, *AURORA*

This ship is a Russian protected cruiser, now preserved as a museum ship in St Petersburg. She became a symbol of the Communist Revolution when she fired the first shots. Laid down in 1896, launched on 24th May 1903 and then commissioned on 29th July 1903, she was finally de-commissioned on 17th November 1948 and made into a museum ship.

Technical specifications:

Displacement of 6,731 tonnes, length 416ft x beam 55.1ft x draught 24ft, speed was nineteen knots with a complement of 578 men. Armament in 1903 was eight x 152mm guns, twenty-four x 75mm and eight x 37mm with three torpedo launchers. Altered in 1917 to fourteen x 152mm, four x 76mm AA, MGs and three torpedo launchers. She was one of three 'Pallada' class cruisers built in St Petersburg for service in the Far East Station. *Aurora* was part of the Russian Pacific Squadron, which was sent from the Baltic to the Pacific. On the way, she sustained light damage from confusing 'friendly' fire in the Dogger Bank incident, then took part in the Battle of Tsushima, but managed to avoid being sunk and with two other cruisers then evaded the Japanese fire and made it to Manila where she was interned. She finally returned to Russia in 1906 and then became a Cadet training ship. She served in the First World War. In 1915 her armament was altered and at the end of 1916 she was moved to St Petersburg (then called Petrograd) for major refitting and repairs. Some of her crew joined in the 1917 Revolution. A revolutionary committee was formed and most of the crew joined in the Revolution. On 25th October 1917, an order to proceed to sea was refused, which sparked off the October Revolution. At 09.45 on that date, a blank shot from her forward turret signalled the assault on the Winter Palace and the crew took part in this attack. There is still some doubt whether this actually took place or if it was a piece of Communist propaganda. In 1922 she was again brought back into service as a training ship. During the Second World War, the guns were removed and taken for the defence of Leningrad. She was docked in Oranienbaum port and badly shelled and bombed and was sunk in the harbour. After extensive repairs in 1945-47, she was permanently anchored on the Neva river in Leningrad (now again St Petersburg) as a monument to the October Revolution and then in 1957 became a museum ship. She was reconstructed in 1984-87 including the replacement of the complete hull below the waterline and also with new funnels and masts. From 1956 to the present time, about twenty-eight million people have visited her in her home berth. On 2nd November 1927 she was awarded the Order of the Red Banner for her revolutionary merits and, on 22nd February 1988, the Order of the October Revolution.

Contact:

Website: http://en.wikipedia.org/wiki/RussiancruiserAurora

Preserved at Sevastopol (Russia) is the Submarine *K21*, and the claim has been made that she torpedoed the German Battleship, *Tirpitz,* but there is no proof whatsoever of this as *Tirpitz* never recorded that she suffered from a torpedo hit.

Plate 156 – Aurora *at sea, 1905. (Image courtesy of Jane's Fighting Ships, 1905 edition.)*

Plate 157 – Aurora *as a museum ship in 2002. (Photo courtesy of Wikipedia)*

Plate 158 – Aurora *in 1903. (Photo courtesy of Wikipedia.)*

B413

Moored at Kalingrad is the Russian submarine *B413*. She is a diesel electric type known as Foxtrot class (project 641). Launched 7th September 1968. Her details are similar to those Russian Subs., that are preserved at San Diego and Long Beach, USA. She served from 1970 to 1990 in the Northern Fleet and visited many countries. From 1991 to 1999 she operated as a unit with the Baltic Fleet. She was decommissioned in late 1999 and transferred to The Museum of the World Ocean.

Contact:

Naberezhnaya Petra Velikogo, 1, 236006 Kalingrad, Russia.
Telephone: 7 4012 34 0244 and 7 4012 53 1744 – Fax 7 4012 34 0211
Email: postmaster@vitiaz.koenig.ru
Website: http://worldocean.ru/en/

GREECE

AVEROF

The Greek battleship *Averof* was commissioned in March 1910.

Technical specifications:

Displacement was 9,450 tonnes, length 462ft x beam 69ft x draught 24.5ft. Guns four x 9.2" x 45 cal, eight x 7.5" x 45 cal, sixteen x 3" (14 pounder), 2 x 3" AA, four x 40mm and two MGs. TTubes were removed. Complement of 670 men. She was preserved and anchored near the Cadet Petty Officers' training school on the Greek Island of Poros, but is now thought to have been moved to Athens.

159

160

Plate 159 – Averof *when in commission in 1910. (Photo courtesy of Jane's Fighting Ships. 1943 official photograph.)*
Plate 160 – Averof *(Photo courtesy of John Rouskas).*
Plate 161 – *The Greek tourist boat* Petrakki *at Corfu Island, an ex-Fairmile 'D' launch. (Photo courtesy of Author's collection.)*

SPAIN

In the Municipal public square at Cartegena lies the preserved Spanish submarine, *Peral* (see Plate 162). This photo shows her as she used to be when she was on display outside the Naval school at Cartegena, but she has now been renovated and is on view in her new setting. She was the first submarine to be offered to the Spanish Navy and was built in 1887. It is named after the inventor and builder, one Lt Isaac Peral, and it was the first ever submarine to have all electric power and so solve this propulsion problem. She was powered by two 420V electric accumulators driving two 30 HP main motors and three auxiliary 5 HP motors for pumping the ballast tanks. She also has a single tube to fire a Schwarzkopf (Blackhead) German torpedo. Perel offered his submarine to the Spanish Navy but they turned it down and in later years they were to regret this decision. She was saved from the wreckers and put on display and has now been moved to her final show place.

162

Plate 162 – Peral *(Author's collection).*

 HOLLAND

THE RAM TURRET VESSEL
SCHORPIOEN

This vessel was one of two built in 1868 at the shipyard, Société des Forges et Chantier at La Seyne-sur-Mer. She was launched on 18th January. She was commissioned by Commander W. K. van Gennep on 17th May and her sea trials were held in the area of Toulon on 16th September. In 1885 – 1886 the three-masted schooner rigging that she carried was dismantled. *Schorpioen* was then put into service in 1887 between the islands of Texel and Ameland to protect the fishing industry there. She was regularly used for training purposes and on 14th February 1903 she was taken out of service in order to be modernised. Although she was built to defend Dutch waters she did once visit a foreign country. In 1871 a squadron was formed on the Scheldt, which comprised six ships, two being *Schorpioen* and her sister ship, *Buffel,* and this squadron went to Antwerp for a visit. On her return to Dutch waters, she carried home the mortal remains of some Dutchmen who had been killed defending the Citadel of Antwerp. She was equipped with only two muzzle-loading cannons of 23cm each. Although built as a Ram Ship, the only time her ram was used was when a merchant ship, the *Maria Adriana*, in 1870 accidentally drifted against her ram and was so damaged that she had to be beached in the vicinity of Brouwershaven. In 1886, she struck the tugboat, *Hercules,* in Nieuwendiep and she sank in the dock where the collision took place. She was repaired and returned to service. She became a depot ship until 1918, when she arrived in Flushing and then on to Germany for two years. Eventually it was decided to scrap her but a group of supporters in Den Helder, where she was moored, attempted to save her but could not raise the money needed, so she could not be saved for that town. In Flushing, where interest had taken hold in the town, it was decided to open a fund to raise the scrap value of the vessel and this was done in the fantastic time of four days. The funds came from trade, industry, retailers, banks and individuals. She was eventually towed from Den Helder to Flushing but got jammed in the Wiegbrub canal for twenty-three hours, but they managed to free her and she entered the dry dock where she now lies (Plate 165). She is now rated as a Maritime Museum and on the top deck there is a restaurant.

Technical specifications:

Length 62.5 metres, breadth 11.58, Draught 4.58. Displacement 2,175 tonnes. Engines two x 2 cylinders, SHP 2,269 = 12.82 knots. Two propellers with two blades each. Crew 135 men. She is armoured and was armed with three Armstrong rifled 23cm cannons, replaced in 1884 by one cannon 28cm, two x cannons 7.5cm, five x cannons 3.7cm but the two cannons of 7.5cm were disposed of in 1895 and since 1907 she has been unarmed.

Contact:

Ramship Schorpioen, Coosje Buskenstraat 56, 4381 LG, Vlissingen, Holland.

Her sister ship, *Buffel*, is also preserved and can be found at Museum Ship Buffel, Leuvehaven, Rotterdam, Holland.

At the time of writing, I have been informed that there is a Dutch Cruiser moored in the canals of Amsterdam, Holland, but I cannot yet get any confirmation of this.

163

164

165

Plate 163 – Dutch Ramship Schorpioen *in dry dock at Flushing. (Photo courtesy of J. B. S. Siwabessy.)*
Plate 164 – The Dutch Ramship Schorpioen *when in service. (Photo courtesy of Marious Bar.)*
Plate 165 – The Dutch Ramship Schorpioen *entering her dry dock berth in Holland prior to her being preserved there. (Photo courtesy of G. Hols.)*

HNLMS *TONIJN* (S805)

At Den Helder, Holland is the Dutch submarine HNLMS *Tonijn*, a Dolfijn/Polvis class boat she was laid down at Wilton Feyenoord Scheidam shipyard, Holland on 26th November 1962. Launched 14th June 1965 and commissioned 24th February 1966.

Technical Specifications:

Displacement was 1,104/1,510 and 1,830 loaded, speed 14.5/17knots, dimensions 79.5 x 7.84 x 4.95. Armament 8/533mm Torpedos (4 fwd 4 aft). Radar equipped, machinery diesel/electric: 2 SEMT – Pielstick 12 PA4V 185 diesels, 1,550 HP each, 2/920 Kw electric motors, two props: 4,400 hp. The exterior hull has three parallel interior pressure cylinders, one of which is on top of two shorter ones. Diving depth was 300m. Had two 169 cell batteries.

The crew and the armament occupied the top cylinder and the batteries and machinery are in the other two. Her sister boat *Dolfjin* was sold for scrap in 1985. *Tonijn* was laid off in 1992 and presented to the Dutch naval museum in 1994 when she opened as a museum ship for visitors.

Contact:

Dutch Naval Museum, Hoofdgracht 3, 1781 AA Den Helder, The Netherlands.
Telephone: 0223 657264 – Fax 0223 657282
Website: http://www.defensie.nl/marine/cultureel/marinemuseum/

HNLMS *ABRAHAM CRIJNSSEN* (A925)

Also at the Dutch Naval Museum with *Tonijn* and *Schorpioen* is the Dutch Van Amstel class minesweeper built by Gusto Shipyard, Schiedam, Netherlands which was launched on 22nd September 1936.

Technical Specifications:

Of 525 tons, 183 x 25.5 x 7 feet, 1 x 3" gun, 4 x 12.7mm AA, 1 MG. After the loss of the Allied ships in the Java Sea battle, she was ordered to make her way to Australia. Her Captain covered her with tree branches and evaded the Japanese fleet. After the war she was employed minesweeping in the East Indies and then returned to the Netherlands in 1951 and was then refitted as a net ship. She was finally decommissioned in 1992 and was used by the Dutch Naval Cadet Corps as a training ship until in 1995 the Royal

Netherlands Naval authorities decided to preserve her as a museum ship. She opened for visitors in July 1997. Her contact details are the same as for *Tonijn*.

Plate 166 – HNLMS Abraham Crijnssen *(Photo courtesy of The Historic Naval Ships Association).*

JAPAN

In the City of Yokosuka is moored the *Mikasa*, a battleship that was the flagship of Admiral Togo and was involved in the War with Russia.

Technical specifications:

She has four x 12" 40 cal, eleven x 6" x 10 cal, twenty x 12 pounder guns. One submerged torpedo tube. She was well armoured, her machinery is two sets x three cylinder triple expansion engines. Two screws. Boilers 25 Belleville. Designed HP 15,000 = eighteen knots. Coal fired with 700 tonnes, maximum 1,690 tonnes. Coal consumption of twelve tonnes per hour at full power. Displacement 15,200 tonnes. Length 415ft (overall 432ft) x beam 75.5ft x draught maximum 27.5ft. She was laid down in 1899, launched in November 1900 and completed in 1902. I have no up-to-date photo of her as my letter to the people who tend her was ignored and returned to me unopened. The above photo is courtesy of Jane's Fighting Ships, 1905 – 1906 and is credited to West.

At Kure is the early Japanese submarine, *Sakuma No. 6,* which had a petrol engine installed and in 1910 she sank after an explosion on board, but was raised in 1920 and was put on display at the Kure Japanese Navy yard as a memorial to the men who were lost in her and is still there to this day.

167

Plate 167 – Mikasa.
*(Photo courtesy of Jane's
Fighting Ships. 1905–06
official photograph.)*

ARGENTINA

Moored in Buenos Aires is the preserved Argentinean cruiser, *Presidente Sarmiento*.

Technical specifications:

She was built at Birkenhead in 1896, and had a displacement of 2,850 tonnes, 251ft x 43ft x 23ft. Had a three x 4.7" 45 cal, one x 4" and two x 6 pounder guns. Three torpedo tubes, coal-fired 330 tonnes, two boilers. Radius 4,500 miles at ten knots. Crew 294. Sheathed and coppered. Built as a training ship for boys, refitted by builders in 1926. Refitted 1940-41 and then put into preservation. More details are unknown due to a letter requesting more details being unanswered.

168 *Plate 168* –
Presidente Sarmiento.
*(Photo courtesy of
Jane's Fighting Ships
1905–06.)*

BULGARIA

In the City of Varna, Bulgaria, is preserved the Torpedo boat, *Deraki*, which sank a Turkish cruiser in 1912. Further information was unobtainable due to a letter not being given the courtesy of an answer by this city.

ITALY

In Rome, Italy, is a torpedo boat, *Mas 15*, of First World War vintage, which is preserved there. Further information unobtainable again due to lack of courtesy of a reply from that city.

CHILE

Another letter that went unanswered is one to the City of Santiago about the former Peruvian Ram Ship, *Huascar*, which was captured by the Chilean ships, *Almiranta Cochrane* and *Blanco Encalade* at the battle of Angmos, thought to be moored at Talca.

POLAND

ORP *BLYSKAWICA* (H34)

At the Naval Museum of Gdynia, Poland, lies the destroyer, *Blyskawica*, which replaced the destroyer, *Grom*, which had deteriorated very badly and was virtually beyond repair.

She was built at the shipyard of John Samuel White in Cowes on the Isle of Wight and commissioned on 25th November 1937.

Technical specifications:

(Dimensions shown in metric)

Displacement standard 2,011 tonnes, full load 2,782 tonnes. Length 114m x width 11.3m x Draught 3.5m. Her top speed was forty-two knots. Turbine rating 54,000 HP, range 3,500 miles at fifteen knots. Crew 200 men. Armament: four x 100mm twin guns, one x 40mm Bofors, three x 37 mm twin AA guns, two x 37mm AA single mount guns, one x 533mm triple TT model 53-39, two x Thornycroft depth charge throwers, two x BMB, two depth charge throwers, two stern release depth charge rails and two x model 08/39 contact mines. She arrived at Gdynia harbour (to be her final resting place) on 1st December 1937. She joined the British Naval forces on 30th August 1939 under Operation 'Peking'. She attacked a U-boat on 7th September 1939 off the English coast and by 1940 was doing convoy duties. She went to the Norwegian Campaign and attacked shore batteries off Narvik and she also was involved at the evacuation of Dunkirk where she rescued the crews of the French *Sirocco* and HMS *Greyhound*. She also defended the Cowes shipyards against the German air raids and on the fortieth and fiftieth anniversary of these raids, the Cowes authorities gave plates to the ship to commemorate these brave acts and these plates can be seen on her on the superstructure astern. In 1942 she was in the Mediterranean, escorting convoys to Malta, and took part in the Allied landings in North Africa and was at Normandy at the landings there. Her last war operation was Operation 'Deadlight' which was the sinking of all the German U-boats that had surrendered at War's end. During the War, she steamed 146,000 sea miles, escorted eighty-three convoys, carried out 108 patrols, sank two ships, damaged three submarines and destroyed four aircraft with a possible three more. She was also considered a 'lucky' ship and though struck three times seriously she had only seven men killed and forty-eight wounded in her war career. On 4th July 1947, she returned to her homeland of Poland to serve as a training unit and after a general repair and refit period in 1969 she became an AA ship. In 1976, she replaced *Burza* as a museum ship and her crew act as guides. On 28th January 1987, the fiftieth anniversary of her service under the Polish flag, she was awarded the highest decoration for bravery, namely The Golden Cross of the Military Order of Virtuti Militari and this is now displayed at an exhibition inside her under the deck.

She is moored in Dock 1 beyond *Skwer Kosciuzki*. She is open for visitors from the beginning of May to the end of November daily except for Mondays and days immediately following holidays. Visiting hours are 10 a.m. to 1 p.m. and 2 p.m. to 5 p.m. Phone: +48 (058) 626-36-58. All these details and photos are courtesy of the Naval Museum at Gdynia and the author would like to take this opportunity to thank all the people concerned at the Naval Museum for their most gracious help to him and the booklets and details they sent.

Plate 169 – *Bow view of ORP* Blyskawica. *(Photo courtesy of Naval Museum at Gdynia.)*
Plate 170 – *Stern view of ORP* Blyskawica. *(Photo courtesy of Naval Museum at Gdynia.)*
Plate 171 – *ORP* Blyskawica *berthed at No. 1 dock. (Photo courtesy of Naval Museum at Gdynia.)*
Plate 172 – *The Golden Cross at Vituti Militari. (Photo courtesy of Naval Museum at Gdynia.)*

FINLAND

THE MUSEUM SUBMARINE *VESIKKO*

Vesikko was built in 1930 as a Vetehinen class boat and was used by the Germans for trials and from which they ordered six of the class from the Crichton-Vulcan boatyard in Turku. This trials boat was named *CV707* and was then purchased by Finland and named *Vesikko* in Autumn 1934 when she joined the Finnish Navy. She was at first used for training but when War broke out between Russia and Finland on 30th November 1939 she patrolled the Gulf of Finland and was then docked in 1940. In June 1941, War again broke out between Russia and Finland and she and her sister boats were ordered to the Eastern Gulf of Finland to patrol. On 3rd July 1941, East of Hogland, she torpedoed the Russian transport ship, *Vyborg*, but due to extensive minefields, her range was limited and she did not sink any more ships. When Russia started its great offensive in the Carelian Isthmus at the beginning of June 1944, *Vesikko* was ordered to the Eastern Gulf of Finland to cover the evacuation of the Finnish army there. Under the terms of the armistice of 19th September 1944 all Finnish submarines were ordered to return to their Naval bases. *Vesikko* made her final voyage as a military vessel in December 1944. In January 1945, the Allied Control Commission ordered the Finnish submarines to be dismantled. The Peace Treaty of Paris (1947) prohibited Finland from keeping submarines and all of them except *Vesikko* were sold as scrap to Belgium in 1953. In 1959, *Vesikko* was conveyed to the Military Museum to be renovated as a museum exhibit. After being cut into five pieces for transportation and then welded together again at the Museum site at Suomenlinna in 1962, she was finally opened to visitors on 9th July 1973.

Technical specifications:

(Dimensions shown in metric)

Dimensions: 40.9 x 4.1 x 4.2 metres, 250 / 300 tonnes, speed thirteen / eight knots, five x 5.3cm torpedoes, one x 20mm AA gun, one x AA MG. Two diesel engines, two electric motors. Range 1,500 miles at ten knots. 150hrs surfaced, fifty miles / four knots, thirteen hours submerged. Crew: twenty.

All photos are courtesy of Vesikko Museum. The author would like to thank the museum for their kind help and information to him.

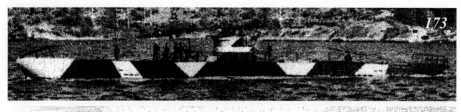

Plate 173 – Vesikko, *camouflaged with depth charge racks in 1942. (Photo courtesy of Vesikko Museum.)*

Plate 174 – Vesikko *at Valmet Ltd's shipyard prior to being cut up and then re-assembled. (Photo courtesy of Vesikko Museum.)*

Plate 175 – *The museum submarine Vesikko dressed overall on the Finnish Navy Day, 9th July 1973. (Photo courtesy of Vesikko Museum.)*

GERMANY

The first German U-boat, the *U1*, can be found in the basement of the German Technical Museum at Munich where it was installed when the building was rebuilt after the Second World War (Plate 176). She was salvaged by her builders in 1919 after she had been put in hand for scrapping and was then preserved, but was damaged by bombing during the Second World War but was able to be repaired. Although numbered U1, she was not the first submarine to be built for the German Navy but the fourth, there being one Holland boat, the *Howalt* and two other unnamed ones, but like these earlier ones, she was built at Kiel in 1906. She was the fourth boat of her class to be built but three were sold to the Russians by the Germania Yard which built them. She was numbered U1 as she was the first submarine of the Imperial German Navy and had a length of 111.3ft with a double hull, and unlike other subs of her time did not have a steam or petrol engine but a Korting heavy oil engine, giving her a surface speed of eleven knots. She had a flat deck casing and a large clipper type bow, which made her more useful on the surface than under it. Two models of her as she was are to be seen displayed in her hull.

At Kiel Naval School is displayed *Le Plongeur Marin* (the sea diver) which was invented by a Bavarian NCO and was built with private money from Kiel citizens at a private shipyard there. She was built because the Danish fleet were blockading the German coast and though she was not very successful, she did serve to make the Danish fleet keep their distance. She is built like a large water tank with a double bottom to allow the water to enter and ballast her down and her trim was then obtained by moving a large ballast weight from stern to stern. In 1851, she sank in Kiel harbour but Bauer, her inventor, managed to escape with two crewmen by allowing her to fill up and equalize the pressure to allow the two hatches to open. The first recorded instance of an underwater escape by pressure equalization! She was re-discovered in 1887 during dredging operations and was then salvaged and refurbished and put on display at Kiel where she still is.

***Plate 176** – German U1 at Munich. (Author's collection).*

MALTA

At Valetta are two ex-British *MTB*s which are run by Captain Morgan Cruises and Am Cruises. One, the *Raia* (AM Cruises), was formerly an MTB, then FPB 1588 and finally Radio Control boat RCB5. The other is named *Ambra* and was of the same Mark II class and they were sold off in October 1958. More details of these craft would be appreciated.

 SWEDEN

At the National Museum of Sweden/the Naval Museum, Stumholmen, Karlskrona are preserved the following warships:

JARRAMAS

The Sail Training Ship *Jarramas* was launched in 1900 at Orlogsvarvet (Navy Yard) Karlskfona, Sweden. She was officially classed as a warship when launched but was relegated to become a sail training ship for the Navy of that time to train cadets and boy seamen in sail work.

Technical specifications:

(Dimensions shown in metric)

Her length is 32.2 metres at the waterline, beam of 8.4 metres and draught of 3.3 metres, her displacement was 300 tonnes (full load) with a sail area of 1,000 square metres. Foremast is twenty-four metres from the deck, mainmast twenty-five-and-a-half from the deck and mizzenmast twenty-five metres from the deck. She carried one hundred cadets and boy seamen plus her normal crew and carried provisions for thirty-five days and water for twenty-eight days. She was de-commissioned in 1950 and then put in hand to be preserved. She remained in service until 1947 when she was replaced by the schooners *Gladan* and *Kalken*. A star on the deck of *Jarramas* denotes that she was a very fast sailer. By Swedish tradition the star was awarded to a sailing vessel that had exceeded sixteen knots. On one occasion *Jarramas* logged 18.3 knots. In 1950 *Jarramas* was sold to the Municipality of Karlskrona and functioned as a tourist attraction and coffee shop until 1997 when she was donated to the Naval Museum on the occasion of the inauguration of the newly-built museum building.

After long and faithful service the *Jarramas* is now in need of total renovation. The 'Save the Jarramas project', which is run by the Naval Museum, is expected to last for five years and cost around SK12 million. On completion of this renovation she will again be seaworthy and fully equipped with everything other than sails. In the future the *Jarramas* will remain moored at the Naval Museum quay where she will play host to a whole range of activities.

Plate 177 – Jarramas
*(Photo courtesy of
Erling Klintefors.)*
Plate 178 – Jarramas
*(Photo courtesy
of Naval Museum,
Sweden.)*

HMS *HAJEN (SHARK)*

This Hajen class of submarine, built to the Holland design, was also built at the Navy yard at Orlogsvarve in 1900. She was the first submarine of the Royal Swedish Navy and was constructed by the Swedish Navy engineer, Garl Richson, who had previously studied J. P. Holland's submarine designs in the US. In 1909 two additional submarines were launched and the *Hajen* thereafter became known as *U Boat No 1*. In 1916 she was modified to update her to the more (then) modern submarines at Bergunds Mekaniske Verkstad yard in Stockholm. The Advance engine was replaced by a diesel motor and she was also fitted with a deck platform (conning tower). She was first commissioned in 1904.

Technical specifications:

(Dimensions shown in metric)

Her length is 23.3 metres with a beam of 3.6 metres and draught of 1.4 metres. She has only a single hull as the early Hollands had and her displacement is about 300 tonnes. She has only one torpedo tube but carried a total of three torpedoes. Her original machinery was kerosene / electric, and was later converted to diesel / electric.

Speed on the surface was nine-and-a-half knots and underwater six-and-a-half knots. Her complement was six officers and twelve ratings. She was finally de-commissioned in 1922 when she was laid up and was then stripped of her machinery and complete inside fittings. Until 1932 she was moored and used for depot duties. She is exhibited at the Naval Museum at Karlskrona and was included into the museum collection already there in 1932. Today she has been refitted with the same exterior as she had in 1916. The latest class of Swedish submarines are also called the Hajen class and there is an HMS *Hajen.*

179

Plates 179 and 180 – HMS Hajan. *(Photos courtesy of Naval Museum, Sweden.)*

180

HMS *BREMON* (55)

HMS *Bremon* is an Arholma class minesweeper built at Eriksbergs yard at Verkstad, Gothenburg, Sweden and launched on 18th June 1940. She is one of a class of twelve minesweepers. These were ordered by Sweden at the outbreak of War in 1939 and although construction was directed from Karlskrona Navy yard, they were built at six different dockyards. They were all named after Swedish Lighthouses.

Technical specifications:

(Dimensions shown in metric)

She was commissioned in 1941 and her length is 55 metres at the waterline, beam of 7.6 metres and draught of 2.1 metres, displacing 450 tonnes. Machinery was steam

turbines, giving 1,600 HP with a speed of seventeen knots. Armed with two x 4.1",
two x 25mm AA and two machine guns. Carried fifty depth charges, forty mines plus
small arms. Minesweeping equipment was paravanes, clearance sweeps and degaussing
equipment. Complement of three officers, seven warrant officers and forty ratings. She
could be employed either as a sweeper or minelayer. Although Sweden was neutral
during the Second World War, mines do not know the difference between friend or foe.
As well as her minesweeping duties, she also acted as a convoy escort and other services
upholding Sweden's neutrality. She was finally taken off the active list in 1966 and
became a training ship in Karlskrona. One boiler and one turbine were kept in working
order and the other opened up for instruction purposes. When steam-powered turbines
were phased out she was put into the Naval Museum in 1987, where she now is.

Plates 181 and 182 – HMS
Bremon. *(Photos courtesy of*
Naval Museum, Sweden.)

TORPEDO BOAT (T38)

This vessel is of the T32 class of torpedo boat, which was an improved version of the
T31 class. Built at Kockums Mekaniska Verksfad boatyard at Malmo, Sweden, she was
launched in 1950 and commissioned in 1951.

Technical specifications:

(Dimensions shown in metric)

Length 23 metres, beam 5.9 metres and draught of 1.4 metres with a displacement of forty tonnes. Her armament was two x 53cm torpedo tubes and torpedoes and four mines or depth charges. Guns were one Bofors 40mm AA, two x M36 mgs, one x 57mm rocket flare launcher. Machinery: Isotta Frashini, 1,500 HP = fifty knots, two x Ford V8 marine = 85HP, speed fifty knots. Complement: five officers and eleven ratings.

At the outbreak of the Second World War in 1939, Sweden realised that she would no longer be able to buy these types of boats from Italy or Britain so she designed and produced them herself. The *T38* belonged to the fourth MTB division at the Galo Naval Base, Stockholm. Following her period of active service, in 1956 *T38* was stripped of her armament and laid up in Karlskrona, until she was finally de-commissioned in 1975. In 1978, *T38* was transferred to the Malmo Museum, Sweden, as an exhibit, but in 1995 she was returned to Karlskrona and the Naval Museum. An extensive restoration project brought her back to her original condition. Since 1998 the *T38* once again sails the waters of the Karlskrona Archipeligo. The vessel is maintained and operated by the T38 preservation Society.

More info: http://www.t38.se

Plates 183 and 184 – T38. *(Photos courtesy of Naval Museum, Sweden.)*

HMS *VASTERVIK* (R136)

This torpedo boat is of the Norrkop (Spica II) class, of which twelve were built and named after Swedish towns. Built and launched in 1974 as a torpedo boat at Karlskrona, Sweden, and commissioned in 1975.

Technical specifications:

(Dimensions shown in metric)

Length 41.3 metres at the waterline, beam of 7.1 metres and draught of 2.4 metres. Displacement nineteen tonnes, armament was (original) six torpedo tubes for 53cm torpedoes, guns one x dual purpose 57mm. Machinery: three Rolls Royce marine Proteus gas turbines = three x 4,500. HP = forty knots. Complement of ten officers and sixteen ratings. In 1982 she was converted into a missile boat and her armament changed to two torpedo tubes and 53cm torpedoes, eight surface-to-surface missile launchers. On this class of boat, the gas turbine exhaust was vented through the transom to provide residual thrust. She was finally paid off and reduced to reserve and then de-commissioned and transferred to the Naval Museum at Karlskrona.

Contact:

The National Maritime Museums of Sweden, The Naval Museum, Sturnholmen, Box 48, SE 371 21 Karlskrona, Sweden.
Telephone: 46 455 35 93 86 – Fax: 46 455 35 93 37.
Website: http://www.maritimuseum.se

I would like to take this opportunity to thank Kristofer Nillson and Annette Telleborn of the Naval Museum for the kind help they have given me in setting up this resume of the Swedish ships that have been well preserved at Karlskrona, Sweden. Also to Erling Klintefors for the photographs used by the museum.

185

Plate 185 *– HMS* Vastervik. *(Photo courtesy of Naval Museum, Sweden.)*
Plates 186 and 187 *– HMS* Vastervik. *(Photos courtesy of Erling Klintefors.)*

NORWAY

ALTA (M314) ex (AMS 104) and *ALRON* (M915)

Moored at Olso is the Norwegian Coastal Sauda class Minesweeper *ALTA (M314) (ex AMS 104 and Alron M915)*. Built by Hodgdon Brothers Shipyard at Maine USA she was launched January 1st 1953 and completed 15th November 1955.

Technical Specifications:

Length 144ft, beam 28ft and draft 8.5ft, with a displacement of 33 tons standard, 384 tons full load. Machinery is GM Diesels, 880 BHP = 13.5 knots. Oil fuel capacity of 25 tons and had a crew of 38.

Originally armed with two x 20mm AA, this was reduced to one only. She served in the US navy as AMS 104 and was then transferred to the Belgian navy being renamed *Arlon (M915)* where she served for a period of 13 years until being taken over by the Norwegian navy in May 1966 in exchange for two ocean minesweepers of the *US MSO* types and renamed *Alta* which is the name of a Norwegian River. There were ten of this class in this navy. This vessel is still in an operational mode and sails about ten to twelve times a year taking visitors and trainees to sea. She is based at Oslo and is under the care of Oslo Maritime Cultural Centre.

Contact:

Aaddress is: Alta Society, PO Box 607 Sentrum, 0106 Oslo, Norway. Ph 47 2255 4388
Email esven@online.no
Website: http://www.knmalta.org.
Address for visits: Olso Maritime Cultural Centre, North Akershus Quay, Oslo, Norway.

PERU

BAP *ABTOA* (SS42) ex *TIBURON*

In Peru is preserved the Abtoa class submarine BAP *Abtoa (SS42* ex *Tiburon)*. Laid down 12th May 1952. Launched 27th October 1953 and completed 20th February 1954.

Technical Specifications:

Of 825 tons (standard) and 1,400 (submerged) she is 243 metres long x 22m x draught 14m. Guns 1 x 5", six x 21" torpedo surface 16 knots submerged 10 knots, radius 5000 miles at ten knots, oil fuel capacity 45 tons and a crew of 40.

She was built with her three sister boats at the Electric boat division General Dynamics Corporation at Groton Connecticut as a modified US *'Mackerel'* class. She is moored at Callao, Peru and is open for visitors.

Contact:

Address: Peruvian Naval Museum, Estacion Naval de Submarinos Base Naval del Calleo, Calleo, Peru.

Telephone: 51 14 42 8707 – Fax 51 14 42 8710.

Email: submarinosperu@speedy.com & museo.abtoa@hotmail.com

Website: http://marina.mil.pe/museocasabapabtao.htm

& http://www.submarinoabtao.com

TURKEY

TCG *ULUCALIREIS* (S338)
ex *USS THORNBACK* (SS 418)

At Istanbul, Turkey lies the Tench class submarine TCG *Ulucalireis S338* (ex USS *Thornback SS 418*). Launched at Portsmouth Naval Shipyard, Portsmouth USA on 7th July 1944 she was commissioned on 13th October 1944. On July 20th, she was decommissioned and converted into a *'Guppy' IIA* class and recommissioned into the US navy on 2nd October 1953. She was finally decommissioned from the US navy on 2nd July 1971 and then transferred to the Turkish navy where she was immediately commissioned. She served for 29 years in this navy and was then decommissioned for the last time and transferred to the museum at Istanbul but remaining the property of the Turkish Navy. Her dimensions are that of the many Guppy class of boats that are preserved in the USA.

Contact:

Address: Rahmi M. Koc. Museum, Haskoy 34445, Istanbul, Turkey.

Telephone: 90 212 369 6600 – Fax 90 212 369 6606

Email: rmkmuseum@koc.com.tr

Website: http://www.rmk-museum.org.tr/

ISRAEL

INS *DABUR*

This Dabur class patrol boat was launched in 1970 at Swiftships Yard, Morgan City, LA, USA.

Technical Specifications:

Dimensions are: 19.7m long, 5.5m beam, displacement of 38tons and a crew of nine. Armed with 2 x 20mm, 2 x 5" Browning Machine guns. Propulsion: 2 x GM diesel engines x 2 propellers at 29 knots.

This class of boats helped in protecting the Israeli coast for some years. The first twelve were made in the USA but later models were built by Israeli Aircraft Industries in the Negev town of Be'er Sheba. During the Yom Kippur War of 1973, they attacked an Egyptian Commando force and destroyed some small craft in their own ports. During the 1980s they underwent overhauls which saw them through the following hectic years. After serving Israel for about 30 years they are being replaced by the new Dvora class of boats.

INS *GAL*

This Gal class of submarine was launched at Vickers yard, Barrow in Farness, UK in 1975.

Technical Specifications:

(Dimensions shown in metric)

Dimensions are length of 45.9m (31m pressure hull) beam 4.7m x 3.8, height 8.8m and displacement of 620 tons on surface, crew of 32. Propulsion of one shaft with 2.85 MW sustained power electric motor, two 16V SE 84 diesel engines with 750kw alternators. Max sped submerged was 17 knots and surface 11 knots, with snorkel raised 9 knots.

After the loss in 1968 of INS *Dakar* with all hands (an ex British T class submarine) Israel decided to buy its next submarines as newly built. The three Gal class (*Gal, Tanin* and *Rahav*) were built with the help of West Germany, UK and Israel. They were built in Vickers Shipyard in the UK. Based on the German *206A sub.*, Israel made changes to suit them. They were small and advanced making them difficult to detect and ideal for coastal missions. They served from 1976 to 2003 and served in several actions especially in the 1982 Lebanon war. They had several upgrades and in 1983 had the UGM 84 harpoon cruise missile installed. In 1987 the newer NT37E torpedos replaced the mark 37s. When the new Dolphin class came into commission in the Israeli navy, the Gal boats were sent to Germany to be sold. The German shipyard then donated Gal to Israel as a museum piece. In October 2007 she was lifted onto a heavy lift ship in Keil and transported to Haifa where she was transferred to a custom built trailer. She is now on exhibition alongside INS *Af Al Pi Chen* and INS *Mivtach* and INC *Dabur*.

Plate 188 – INS Gal
(Photo courtesy of Historic Naval Ships.)

INS AF AL PI CHEN

This vessel is an ex British WWII landing craft (tank) launched on 23rd September 1941 at Stockton Construction Co's shipyard at Thornaby UK.

Technical Specification:

(Dimensions shown in metric)

Length 48.5m, beam 9.1m with a loaded displacement of 700 tons (empty 300 tons). Armament 2 x 2lb pom poms for AA use plus some machine guns. Propelled by three diesel engines, 16 cylinder 150 hp = 7 knots.

She was completed in December 1942 and later was converted at Portsmouth UK to a Landing Craft Rocket ship. She could fire approximately 1,000 rockets and carried five reloads. In June 1943 she was moved to the Mediterranean and was used during the invasion of North Africa. She was finally paid off from the British fleet in May of 1945. In 1946 she was sold to the Italian fleet and later was sold on to a shipping company and renamed Michael Parma. In 1946 she landed up in the control of 'Mosad le Aliyah Bet' who were resisting the British forces and their immigration quotas. She sailed just after the 'Exodus' episode in 1947. She was named after this event which means 'Nevertheless' or 'In spite of it all'. On the 17th September 1947 she left Formia, Italy with 434 persons aboard but whilst heading to Palestine, she was detected by a British aircraft and then intercepted by four destroyers. She then rammed one of the destroyers but the British put boarding teams on her and she was then towed to Haifa Bay. The people were put into internment camps in Cyprus and most of them eventually made it to Palestine. In June 1948 when the British mandate expired the new Israeli Navy was looking for ships and found her and she participated in the 1948 Independence celebrations as a navy training ship. In 1956 she briefly became a LCT once more when it was decided to push her by tug (her engines were useless) to land tanks near Gaza in Operation Musketeer but she was not needed after all. She was decommissioned in 1958 and in 1968 was moved ashore and became a museum ship in the Haifa navy museum

Plate 189 – INS Af Al Pi Chen *(Photos courtesy Clandestine Immigration and Navy Museum.)*

INS *MIVTACH*

This vessel of the Sa'ar class was built in France by the Construction Mec. De Normandie at Cherbourg and launched in April 1967 being finished in June 1968.

Technical Specifications:

Of 22 tons (250 full load) and a speed of 40 knots she is 45m long x 7m wide x 1.8m draught. Originally armed with 3 x 40mm guns and in 1974 was re-armed with 2 x 40mm, five Gabriel missiles and 3 x ASW torpedos (mark 44/46) Hull mounted sonar, 4 x diesel engines, 16v cylinder 3500hp.

On 25th December 1967 she sailed to her home port of Haifa. During her service life she was actively involved in anti terrorist activities and also in the Yom Kippur war. She was finally laid off and decommissioned in January 1996 and made a museum ship at Haifa where she is ashore mounted upon a cradle.

All of these ships are of the Clandestine Immigration and Navy Museum,

Contact:

204 Allenby Street, Haifa 35472, Israel.

Telephone: 04 8536249 – Fax: 04 88512958.

Website: http//www.amutayam.org.il

ACKNOWLEDGEMENTS

Now that I have come to the end of the material that I have gathered on these lovingly restored ships, I would again like to thank all those generous people who have helped me by sending me material when I requested it. For those who ignored me or did not reply, then thank you for nothing. I would like to say 'Thank you very much indeed' to the following sources: USA Navy Office of Information; The US Battleship Commission; The State of Massachusetts and their Memorial Committee; The Alabama Battleship Commission; Battleship Texas Commission; Commonwealth of Pennsylvania; Cruiser Olympia Association; Patriots' Point Development Authority; The Aircraft Carrier Hornet Museum for their extra help; City of Galveston; Great Lakes Navy Association; The Manitowoc Maritime Museum of Hackensack Memorial Association; Chicago Museum of Science; Louisiana State Museum; New London Submarine Base; Patterson (NJ) Museum; Jason Hall of Battleship, New Jersey; The Washington Naval Memorial Museum; The British National Historic Ships; the Trincomalee Trust; Chatham Historic Dockyard; Philip Simons of Portslade; and also Nick Hall for the Shoreham photos; British Military Powerboat Trust; The Maritime Museum of Australia; HM Canadian Ships, *Haida* and *Sackville*; City of Melbourne Council; John Rouskos of Greece; Ramship Schorpioen Trust; The Polish Naval (Gdynia) Museum; The Finnish Vesikko Museum; and The Munich Museum; National Maritime Museum of Sweden, and all the other many people who have given me such great help in these several years of study and research. In the event of any other preserved vessels that I have not mentioned through having no knowledge of them, then, I apologise, please send me the details. Finally, to my very great friend, Mike Neary, who has kept my printer supplied with cartridges and ink for several years without complaint, and has kept me going through ill health with his support, I say "Thanks, Mate, you're the best pal a bloke could have, and I dedicate this book to you with my grateful thanks."

To a lovely lady (who wishes to remain anonymous) I also would like to say a grateful "Thank you" for your help.